Purposefully Woven

Turn Tragedy & Trial into Triumphs

live with purpose. ♡ *Kele*

Kele Pandolfe

Purposely Woven

Purposefully Woven

PUBLISHED BY KELE PANDOLFE

Requests for information should be addressed to kelesue28@gmail.com

Trade Paperback ISBN 978-0-359-45172-2

Cover design by Kele Pandolfe

Unless otherwise marked, scripture quotations are taken from the ESV Bible (The Holy Bible, English Standard Version)

Ordering Information: Special discounts are available to those ordering in bulk quantities. For details please message the author at kelesue28@gmail.com

Printed in the United States of America 2019 – First Edition

Dedication

To my mom, who weaved into my fabric, the importance of saturating my heart & mind in Gods Word. Your example of strength through adversity caused me to seek from where that strength came. Actions speak SO much louder than words. Thank you for modeling and imparting a rich eternal legacy to me. I Love you!

Purposely Woven

Contents

Purposely Woven

Foreword

The question of pain and suffering is one that every human being must eventually face. This is because, quite simply, pain and suffering are an ambiguous part of the human experience. These struggles can enter our lives for a variety of reasons. Sometimes struggles are a result of our own sinful choices. Other times they come our way because of the sinful choices of others. At still other times, we struggle simply because of the broken and fallen state of the world in which we live.

Although it feels almost instinctual to cover ourselves and hide in the midst of our sufferings, it is always to our benefit to instead turn to our Lord, immerse ourselves in His word, and take solace in His people. Writing with a wisdom born out of her own times of pain and suffering, this is exactly what Kele encourages us to do. In the telling of her own

Purposely Woven

story, it's as if Kele manages to walk alongside each of us in ours. She is real, reliable, and relatable as she firmly directs us to the only one who can fully and finally "restore, confirm, strengthen and establish" us.

In a world where we have the ability to carefully curate every image of ourselves by passing it through a dozen filters before we hit "post", I take heart knowing a woman like Kele, who so openly shares the brokenness and beauty of her own story without any filters at all.

I pray Kele's story and words will lead you to the mighty God she so humbly serves.

Summer Lacy

Author, Speaker, Bible teacher

www.HisWordAlone.com

Acknowledgements

I would like to thank my support team at Do Good Ministries, who without your support and prayers this book would not exist.

To Debbie, Jennifer and Karen for sharing your path from broken to beauty with me, to pour into others. To Kelly, I am so thankful God wired your brain different than mine girl, then chose to interweave our paths.

To my Abba. You knit, know and guide me. My purpose is so clear, yet the journey to get there known, only to you. The daily knitting you commit to my minutes and for "knowing me", to depths I will most likely never comprehend.

As you guide, I pray I see the colors you weave and obediently hear the melody you sing upon my steps

Introduction

I would like to say this right out the starting gate, girls: I am a hot mess! I have a history of sin, mistakes, heartbreak, and failure. So if you were looking for someone who could tell you her life is or has ever been sin and mess free, then you better close this book and scour the shelves for another because these pages will *not* tickle your ears with such fancy! What comes with my spectacularly messy story is beautiful redemption. Mine is a story still being written, yet already filled with heroic rescue, covered in grace, smothered with love, and set free! So, if you're looking for *that* kind of story, then get ready to turn some pages with me.

Let's begin, well, at the beginning. I was a twelve-year-old girl abandoned by the first man whose job it was to love and protect her. A young woman of sixteen looking to fill that void, making poor choices, pregnant, and scared. A proud mamma whose dream in life was nothing more than to be one, found herself feeling exhausted, unnoticed, and unappreciated. A middle-aged mother of three teens living in a marriage of broken vows.

As my story unravels, you will find tangles in the tapestry, some created by my poor choices, some manipulated in the hands of others who did not handle my making with care. The weaving is made of people, places, and decisions. My tapestry is woven with dark colors, bright colors, and some colors that are only yet to be seen. But it is my story, one whose colors tangle carelessly, coupled with blank areas waiting to be finished. You, too, my friend, have a story. You have a tapestry of life being craftily woven with your own colors as each day passes. To weave is to intertwine, to bind. It takes delicate time and attention. During this weaving process, you will encounter snags along the way, left there for you to tangle or to unravel. There are days when the unraveling is difficult and other days

Purposely Woven

when the weave is a perfect fit, filled with colors of blessing and joy, creating your story, your masterpiece! My story is sprinkled with grace, soaked in God's redemption, and secured over and over by the *only* One who can mend each snag, fill holes, and bind up the frayed edges. There is such beauty in our mess, my friend! Yes, beauty.

This book was birthed from pain, heartbreak, and trials that are still alive and well today, weaving vibrant colors and patterns into my tapestry. I believe my mess is a message. Trials have the ability to break us or to make a masterpiece! Sometimes it just takes the gentle task of unraveling the brokenness and hurt that have weaved their way into our very fabric. This is a journey in learning to untangle–to wrestle with regret, disappointment, unworthiness, and the burden of defeat. We have a choice, a choice to weave the brokenness and heartbreak into our tapestry for the gift it is and to intertwine the colors of freedom through our greatest failures! Will you join me on this journey? Into the reality that we are *all a*

Hot Little Mess! The best news is, though we are broken, we are beautiful. Woven for a purpose, cared and crafted for by the most capable hands.
Kele

The Weaving Process

Indulge me here as the history nerd I am! I just love to see how things were done the days before I walked this earth. I love to learn about the people before me – how they lived, learned, worked. I am fascinated at how simply they lived compared to how complexly we do. Yet there are certain things socially and physically that are the same. We live in a time where we are the most connected to each other than we have ever been and at the same time the most disconnected. We don't even know the names of the women that live right down the street. That's a whole other book though, sister! Don't get me started.

Going back just 100 years, we can see the vast difference in home life, marriage, morals, and values. Even though things have changed over the decades on a monumental scale (not for the better in most cases), there are timeless skills that have not. Weaving tapestry is one of them. Yes, the process is done on a quicker timeline, but the story of the weaving and how it is accomplished are the same. Speeding up the process can diminish the quality of the weaving. It takes care and patience to weave a tapestry into the picture story it was imagined to be by its artist.

It all begins with a single artist who draws and imagines the picture or dimensions to be created. The weaver then takes over and interprets that creative imagination into a grand masterpiece. Everything from the surface to be marked to the colors chosen is selected with the utmost care and proficiency by the artist. Materials are chosen very carefully. Wool for strength. Silk for illumination. Silver or gold for wealth and regency. The weaving process goes from artist to dye master. The strands that make tapestry are called *weft*. They are woven strand by strand to make a fabric picture. The process to dye each strand is magical. Dye must be carefully measured and weighed to an exact number to match colors. The dye bath is then heated to a perfect temperature, the weft soaked for hours in this, colorful concoction. After the allotted time, the weft is then carefully examined to make sure the color is vibrant and matches the artist's sketch. If it is not quite ready or needs more matching, more dye is added, and more soaking time is needed. When ready, the weft is wound onto a broche (or spool) for storage, waiting for the weaver's hand to manipulate. When the weaver is ready to use the weft, it is then transferred from the spool to the weaver's tool. The weaver has already prepared the warp, which is a vertical tapestry of thick strands. Each warp is prepared according to the weaver's specific specifications, formed from one single thread, and wound to make a continuous vertical tapestry base in which the weft will be woven into. Once the length is right, the warp goes through a process of tightening and loosening over and over until the weaver is satisfied with the base for the tapestry. It must be just perfect for the weaver to begin weaving the colors of the weft.

The weaver has complete control and investment from beginning to end of the tapestry weaving creation. As each color of the weft is intermingled into the warp base, the weaver sits behind the creation being formed, facing the back of the tapestry, adding threads of color while weaving. All the colors are there, left hanging so the weaver can intermix colors when needed. While weaving, the weaver will occasionally look through the warp to see the front of the tapestry in a mirror. When the mirror is placed just right, the woven and warp area match just perfectly. Through the weaving process, the warp is covered up completely by the colorful weft in a series of left-right and up-down motions. What is birthed from this creative, imaginative, laborious task is a celebration, a work that honors the artist, the weaver, and all who intermingled to create it!

Like a tapestry, each of *us* is a creation, formed from the innermost thoughts of our creator. From a tiny nugget to roly-poly bundle, we are birthed into a world that begins shaping us from hour one. We do not choose our birth place, family, or position as a child. We are placed where the Master Artist and Weaver imagines us. Our surfaces are carefully marked and followed by Him. Colors are painstakingly picked and dyed to exact specifications from the Artist's mind. The strands that are meant to form us are for strength, illumination, and spiritual wealth. As our colors form, they can be vibrant and beautiful mixed with a mystical depth. We are tempered, matched for sustainability, carefully measured. As our Weaver winds us with all we are and who He imagines us to be, we form, are refined. What will become of these colors, these strands? As our stories begin, we are continuously winding new colors—some color choices are ours and some colors are chosen for us by others that intermingle into our strands.

This tapestry of ours has a base which we attach our colors to, waiting for other colors to intertwine. Without it, each strand would just fall to the floor beneath, forgotten. Sometimes the weaving is silky and easy; sometimes knots and tangles are formed. New colors are added, carefully picked up by the Weaver and placed to perfection into each master strand. The Weaver is merciful, yet bold with the color placement. The careful attention to detail and wisdom in the Weaver's control over this process is remarkable. The investment the Weaver has into our creation is incomprehensible.

The point here, my friend, is we *are masterpieces*. You may not feel very colorful. You may even feel like your colors and threads are so ugly or useless that they are better off in the scrap pile to be burned. Friend, I feel your heart and pain. The process to become all the Master Weaver intends us to be can take longer for us than others. The pain or rejection we suffer at times can threaten to cripple the story that was meant to be ours. Can I encourage you to remember that the Weaver is seated right behind you with His hand on your strands? Careful not to neglect one thread. He is peaking through the weaving, continuously righting every misplaced

Purposely Woven

color or thread. He has His eye carefully focused right now on what colors are being placed where, so that the final creation is just as He imagined. I encourage you to not rush the process but to let Him have the control within your weaving so that as your life tapestry comes to life, you can celebrate the honor and beauty that flows from it.

One

My Weaving

"Wait for the Lord, be strong and let your heart take courage; wait for the Lord."
Psalm 27:14

My face was pasted to the floor, the taste of salty tears dripping down. Heavy sobs came from a depth I had no idea existed within me, sounds that could not possibly be coming from *my* mouth. My heart ached – no, not ached – was ripping into minute pieces by the realization of a separation so painful the tearing could be felt like the ripping of flesh from bones. I watched it happen with no power to stop it! You know the cliché we have all been known to say when we see something terrible –

Purposely Woven

"Oh, that's heartbreaking." This word *heartbreak*—it has a meaning, a depth, a weight to me now.

This moment was one of many to come for me. This *first* one was my moment of realization, a reality that would be my tomorrow because a 20-year relationship had been broken, abandoned, forgotten, and replaced. I had prayed for healing. Cried for help. Begged to be heard. I thought—I mean really believed—that I had given this over to God. Why was I shocked by this outcome? The signs were there for years. Was I to blame for the lies and behavior that became a constant third-party companion? Could I have prayed harder? Accepted harmful behaviors and sin with more welcome? Of course, these thoughts swirled through my head as my adult son wept in my arms after confronting the evil that had taken root and broken the bonds of "family." He begged for restoration of the familiar

– to choose him, me, us. Could I have been wiser, more faithful, skinnier...better? Would any of that have made a difference?

As you are reading this, chills may swarm your spine with the familiarity of my circumstances. The ache of it may reach your core, or you may have felt these very thoughts and feelings for reasons of your own. It could be a prodigal child, an illness, a diagnosis, harsh words spoken to you over and over by a "loved" one, a death, or pain from your childhood, do to abuse or abandonment. Maybe it's a broken friendship or unemployment. Maybe its regret – sins for which you can't seem to forgive *yourself*. The list is endless, and the aftertaste is poison in your mouth, slithering deep into your soul!

My heartbreak was years in the making. I saw it coming – years of lies, addiction, and deceit that I would address head-on one day but then tuck away the next when the unbearable pain of facing it interfered with "doing life." This was also not the first heartbreaking traumatic experience for me. Abandonment was a constant norm, an unwelcome friend, beginning at a young age. So, when I found myself lying prostrate on the floor, face wet by tears, heart torn into uncollectible pieces, the questions I had to ask were, "How will I begin the monumental task of reconstructing every piece? Do I even want to pick myself up and move on?"

As we dive into these answers, I have included a special treat for you! I have had the honor to have met some remarkable women through my journeys around the sun so far. These women have walked painful, beautiful stories of their own – some very different and some hair-raisingly similar to mine. I wanted to introduce some of them to you so that you too can marinate in their wisdom gained from trials they have faced. We are all on this journey together. I pray we can learn more from each other's pain, rather than compare or judge each other. I know I have been mightily blessed by these precious women, and I pray you are, too. I asked questions about their healing and placed their answers at the back of the book under "Chapter Questions." Whether you refer to them after each chapter or wait to read them at the end, I pray that as I share my friends with you, you are reminded that we are *never* alone. God brings beautiful people into our lives who cross our paths at the very moment He intends. I am reminded of this very fact every time I sit across from one of "my people" through a cup of "coffee talk," as they hold my hand in prayer or wipe my tears as I weep through heartache. Don't underestimate the power of God's timing and whom He chooses to place before you. I for one am a better friend, daughter, mother, and woman because of these encounters.

Purposely Woven

List the 2-3 women in your life who can speak TRUTH & LIFE into you.

What are your broken pieces to be collected? (Use the space below to write)

Purposely Woven

Choosing the Weave

"Therefore, the LORD waits to be gracious to you, and therefore He exults himself to show mercy to you. For the LORD is a God of justice; blessed are all those who wait for him." Isaiah 30:18

The glory dwelling inside of our brokenness is that we have choices. Broken things only stay broken when we leave them there on the floor to take up space, clutter our lives, and endanger us with their sharp debris. When we choose slowly, gingerly, to pick up the tiny pieces—every shard and chunk, not missing a single sharp or dull edge—mending can then begin. This will be time consuming, tedious, and soul shaking, yet as we choose to face the broken mess before us, we choose the task of unraveling. We unravel our tangles to continue the weaving of our tapestry! To live alive and with purpose is to live in seasons of salty tears, mascara-lined cheeks, cracked, then taped together hearts, and difficult relationships that require our prayers and a lot of attention. This is a life alive and abundant. It is life right where you are, when all your glory intertwines with your brokenness.

I have been broken, pieced back together, and then dropped again throughout my 42 years – more than I would like to admit to the girl that looks back at me in the mirror. Yet I have come to learn that each heartbreak and tangled thread has brought me here, brought me to this hour, facing this new day. It's not the social-media-profile-Christmas-card-picture life. It's a life with a whole lot of messy colors reflecting its rays.

My story is also *planned* and *known*. Mine is a well-crafted story that I can't even begin to imagine or plan. So is yours, friend! Each of our lives is carefully molded, wisely directed, and handled with the utmost care. Now, I know you might be thinking, "But you don't know what I have endured, what my heart has been put through." You are right! I will never presume to know your heartbreak or pain, yet we were all created by the One who does. Stick with me here. Don't shut this book and move on thinking, "You just don't know..." I pray that the pain I have endured through the years was for a purpose. God gave me these words to write to you. My prayer, as you and I choose to mend, is that we see the gift we are given through each trial that we look through the pain and *choose* to see the great responsibility that comes along with pain and suffering. By choosing to weave the glory into it, we choose to live abundant hours instead of defeated days. Choose to move from just existing to really living. Choose to step out of survival mode, to a life that seeks purpose, not just existence. We then, leave behind lives filled with bitterness, hurt, pain, and heartbreak and enter days focused on finding the *why* in the mess and the *how* in moving forward into healthy, abundant life. We choose to live with pep in our step and the drive to move ahead with so much passion and purpose that it would take a herd of hippos to stop us!

As we plunge into this healing process, please know I am reading, praying, healing right along with you. Healing is not a destination but a wondrous journey, intertwining each colorful thread God offers us. Thank you for being brave, for seeing that the choice to mend needs to be made in order for healing to begin.

There is no chart or cookie-cutter way to grieve or to heal from hurt and loss. We were created by a Master Weaver who made our every fiber, fashioned us with emotions, and constructed each brain wave. So this means He knows better than anyone how to mend what's broken. His Word is a balm to our very souls if we let it saturate us. What a gift we have that the Creator of all things chooses to give the power of healing and mending to what evil intends to rot!

Over the next pages, let's learn to tackle this gift of grief. For if we never break we will never know what it means to be whole. This in my opinion is one of the most overlooked areas of loss. I am sure there are many of you holding this book who have experienced physical death of a loved one. That is loss on a scale with unsurmountable weight, my friend. Death leaves a vacant space your beloved once occupied. Death comes in other forms, as well, such as death of a relationship or an image, death in the form of losing one's self to things or people that may be toxic, or death of a dream or a reality. My point here is this: death wears many faces, and if we suppress our feelings and don't face reality by thoroughly grieving, we are doing ourselves a grave injustice. The resurfacing of what has died will bubble up in other avenues of this life journey. Those bubbles will turn into floods of water whose aim will be to drown your purpose. Let's not wade in that water, friend. Let's choose to brave the storms of grief. When we can begin the task of peeking through the curtain to face our monsters, then, and only then can we really start the refining process that is so imperative to living fully.

Purposely Woven

What are the "deaths" in your soul that you have experienced on your journey so far?

_____

_____

_____

_____

Write out Psalm 119:27.

Purposely Woven

Meditation is "Continued or extended thought; reflection; contemplation." I call it studying deep! There are many things vying for our attention every minute of each day. We live in the most technologically advanced era, yet we are the most disconnected generation on many levels. The point here is, we make hundreds of choices daily, from the food we eat, to the clothing we wear, to where and on whom we will focus our time and talents. It is important that we choose to meditate (study deeply) on God's Word. In this verse the writer is asking – no, *choosing* to ask – for understanding of things that are hard, that are unimaginable. When we are thirsty and in want it catapults us into a deeper want for that "thing". I pray that each of us "thirst" deeply for His word and what it speaks to our lives.

Take some time writing out a prayer today, a prayer that asks to understand His Word. The truth behind it, and its wondrous works. This, my friend, is a huge step in choosing. A giant leap in coming out of the pain and hurt and choosing to see it for something brighter and grander than what you have boxed it to be. God is waiting to unwrap your box and show you the marvelous gift it can be.

Three

Unraveling Grief

"Be still and know that I am God, I will be exalted among the nations, I will be exalted in the earth! The LORD of hosts is with us; the God of Jacob is our fortress." Psalm 46:10-11

Grief—I firmly believe it never ends, but changes. Grief is a journey that twists and turns until we decide we are not going to take that turn again and choose to derail. It is not a place we should pitch our tents for long stays. Grief is not a sign of weakness or lack of faith. It is a very dear price we pay when we choose to invest in others, to love and to become vulnerable. *Grief*—the word itself carries a heaviness to it, a weight that seems just too burdensome to bear along the journey. Grief can also be overlooked as "just the way it is." We are so quick to brush it to the side and move forward. Do we really move forward, though?

I used to think grief was weakness. I really did not see the need to grieve over injustices done to me. I was taught as a child to put on my "big girl pants" and deal with it: "If you're not dying or bleeding, then keep moving." So when it came to heartbreaks and pain, I just thought, "Well, Kele, get over it. Everyone goes through it." Don't get me wrong here. We all have had disappointments and expectations that go unmet, which are inconvenient, or may push our day off kilter a bit. These are not the circumstances of grieving I am talking about. These we are speaking of are raw, open wounds that require a sensitive touch. Loss so deep it hollows out a portion of our very being. Trauma so saturated into the mind and body, that there are daily reminders of painful past experiences. A shock to our souls that will forever require our attention.

Grief creates anger that cannot easily be brushed away. Bitterness and depression can become constant companions that cohabitate quite nicely. Denial and loneliness are friends we keep close. This, my friend, is grieving. If you're anything like me, you had no idea that you were walking a path straight through the big "G." I thought I was handling all my broken pieces just fine. It's perfectly normal to cry, right? To have a pity party occasionally? Yes, it is, but as I started to feel (excuse my language) pretty pissed off, I started to see how my handling this business of grief on my own was making a much bigger mess along the journey.

As I went along searching for some clarity and sanity through the fog, I opened my Bible and went into the Word. I became aware of truth within my pain, the truth that there is undeniable healing in those dark hours and seasons of grief. I was awakened to the necessity of this healing journey for my future. Grief became a way of relating for a season. I started to see my situation as opportunity, not a burden. I saw in it the potential to grow me, not to break me.

Learning to grieve properly is painful and time-consuming. Yet the freedom that is birthed from it is something you cannot explain to another. I started to learn how to let each stage I encountered be raw and real. Depression was not a part of who I was, not in one fiber of my being, but when I found myself dipping into a world of great loss – into vacant and lonely spaces – I could either put on my "selfie face" or pretend all was good, ignoring the critical issues that plagued. Or I could bear down and be real with my innermost thoughts. Be open and vulnerable. Dip into the

Purposely Woven

shallow end of the messy muck that was left to settle on the shore of my soul. It takes courage to see the beauty that can blossom through this process.

Here's the thing: if we choose *not* to grieve through this—if we choose to put on our happy face, convincing ourselves we are better off just going another day pretending —we simply stuff the pain into a tiny box that sits on a shelf in our soul, teetering right on the edge, ready to fall and expose its rotting contents. By choosing to tuck it away, we miss out on what God wants to teach and show us and set ourselves up for a bigger mess to clean up down the road.

I am convinced that we in our modern society have been given the curse of instant gratification—from food so fast we complain when we must wait more than two minutes at the pick-up window to (I'm guilty of this one) when we order online, "Why don't they have free two-day shipping? You mean I must wait!?" Instant gratification has taught us that anything that takes more than 10 minutes of our attention is an inconvenience, not worthy of our time or attention. It sucks the truly valuable things from us. Oh, how wrong we are! God created us for relationship, not only with Him but with others, and that, my friend, can get uncomfortable and messy! These uncomfortable moments are sometimes years in the making, yet we expect them to be healed at lighting speed.

The journey through grief is where the transformation begins. To *transform* means to *"change form or condition, nature or character, to convert or metamorphose."* I love that! If we are to be changed in this process, then we are to go through a transformation process, a metamorphosis through grief. As we grieve, we heal. As we heal, we transform. As we transform, we metamorphose into creatures that we had no comprehension existed underneath the hurt. Let's get going, friend!

Each step of grieving may or may not apply to you in your season, and not everyone will live them in "order." The beauty is, God knows your innermost pain and secrets. He has woven your past and is weaving your future, still. He will break through and heal each grieving heart that seeks His face!

Are you ready to go through the process of grieving? What is or has been lost in your life? What is your hope in this conversion or metamorphosis?

Purposely Woven

Four

Unraveling Denial

"Therefore, confess your sins to one another and pray for one another,
that you may be healed. The prayer of the righteous person has great power as it
is working." James 5:16

"It's ok, it will get better." I can attest to this one. I was camped out here for years. I was in denial that addiction and unfaithfulness were living breathing entities in my most important relationship. I knew it was there but chose to rationalize it. I made an image in my mind of what could be instead of what was. This, my friend, is normal. Denial is normal–yes, normal! We have been taught that denial is a negative thing; however, denial is one way our mind naturally protects us from experiencing more pain. I was convinced that someday the other parties would realize the damage this behavior was causing, that they would "choose the better, the right." It's an important protective function that cannot be glazed over in the grieving process. I knew in my heart that the father of lies and deceit was living in my home, but I was telling myself all the lies I needed to believe just to make it work. See, if I could stay in this denial, then I wouldn't have to feel the pain of what was in truth a failing marriage.

Denial is a process we have to heal through, not demand things from. Ignoring it will not make it go away either. It takes time for us to fully comprehend just what it is that sits before us in the pool of denial. I found an interesting truth in my own life as I muddled my way through my denial. I wanted so badly the image of what could be that I was blinded by the reality of what was. As we start to stare denial smack dab in the face, we will begin to see that the "what" we wanted to see may not be what God is asking us to pursue. He has a passion and purpose beyond our mess; we are just not seeing it, not when we are drowning in the cesspool of denial. Once we can move through this stage of grief in God's mercy and kindness, we can then come out of the fog, maybe not *fine* but *functioning* and able to see through the haze into a new reality. When we feel the haze lift, we will be able to call the monster by name, clearly see the terrain we came through to get there, and thereby see the pain for what it is, not what we painted it to be in order to make daily life more manageable.

God will meet us right where we are, *not* where we pretend to be! He is a God of truth and justice. He exposes that truth in our hearts because

He loves us and wants us to see the beauty in living life to its completeness in Him. Living any other way is robbing us of His redemptive plan for our lives and depriving God of the glory that is rightly due Him. He wants us to see that His justice will always be brought forth. Yet, if our minds and hearts are holding on so tightly to the noose of denial, we will be choked out by it. Let's look at some verses that will help us tackle this painful season. You may want to use a journal or the spaces below.

Look up and write out each scripture:

Matthew 5:4 _____

_____

_____

Purposely Woven

Psalm 73:26 _____

_____

_____

How do you feel your heart and flesh are failing?

_____

_____

_____

_____

Psalm 107:13-15 _____

_____

_____

What darkness are you in today? What bonds do you feel placed upon you?

_____

_____

_____

_____

Psalm 34:18 _____

_____

_____

Purposely Woven

We are told that the Lord is near to you when you have a broken heart. Write out the areas in which you feel broken. We are also told that when our spirit is crushed, He saves us. How is your spirit crushed today?

As we face this monster, denial, we will start to recognize distortions and see people and or situations for who or what they are, not what we want or hoped they would be. Pain, situations, confused thoughts. Make so much more sense. We can start to accept what our role was or is in the relationship or situation and start taking ownership of OUR truth, not truth the others may have pressed upon us in shame. When we can start to unravel and believe that we cannot control others or convince them to make a decision that would be best for all involved, we take ownership of truth, and the freedom in that is exciting! You release yourself of their sin, wipe clean the shame and guilt of not being enough and take all those *nots* – not wise enough, not thin enough, not good enough (enter yours here) – you placed upon your shoulders and give them over to God. He has big shoulders and will willingly take it all!

Being honest with yourself when an injustice is committed against you or the ones you love is not only freeing but also necessary to grieving. Cry! Let others see you cry! Oh, snap, that just almost sent you into an anxiety attack right there! But for real, girl. We are all in this tapestry of life together. We all need to stop the charade of perfectionism. God chose to eat and fellowship with the "least of these." If that's whom He is using, then sign me up! I want to be raw and exposed so healing can begin. We have the choice to face our monsters with the Creator of the universe at our side. I want Him on my fighting squad, don't you? Understand that as we work through this denial process, there is absolutely no time frame, nor are there boxes to check. No, ma'am, this is between you and your Creator. As you give it to Him, He will make a balm for your heart and soul, slathering it on at the perfect time. So let's go in prayer and do this! To be able to abide in Christ means being *with* Him. Talking to Him. This will look one way for you and another for me. I might rise early and spend quite time with Him. Sharing, listening, crying, and giving Him all my questions, adoration, or requests. You might snuggle in after a long day and a freshly washed face under the covers of night and spend that time.

There is no *right time*. Talking to Him is so very personal, in time I pray this time becomes your normal. Your everyday drinking that you need to wrestle through. Just "come" friend, just come, from a well so deep, you come day after day. Some days you will just sit and hear His voice speak love, truth and mercy upon you. Others, you may come ready for battle, with wrestling unanswered.

Purposely Woven

Please grab your journal or use the space below to write a prayer to God. By the end of this book, if your journal is anything like mine, it will have tear stains and crinkled pages. Lay it *all* out, giving it to Him.

Five

Unraveling the Bargain

"In all your ways acknowledge him, and he will make straight your paths. Be not wise in your own eyes; fear the LORD and turn away from evil." Psalm 3:6-7

"If you could just heal me (my spouse, my child, my sister...) Lord." "If you will please bring my husband (my child, my loved one) home again." "If you could take this pain away from me, heal this hurt..." Oh, friend, I can admit to you today that I have most certainly spoken a few of these pleas! Of course, we want to be healed, saved, loved, found, reunited... but why do we feel the need to bargain? If you are anything like me, these thoughts can just slip out of your mind and into your prayer time.

Bargaining is most often birthed from fear and confusion. Why is it so important to our grieving process? For a couple of reasons: it gives our minds temporary escape from the pain, and it is another way for our mind to protect itself from the deep feeling of loss that we are not quite ready to own up to. We want to just stay put for a few more moments, days, or even years, pretending if we just try one more time, we may be able to find another angle around the pain or loss. It gives us time to adjust to our new circumstance. To see this new normal as our new reality.

God is a God of order and of timing. We have our own time table, but God has His, and if you have lived more than 10 minutes on this planet, then you can see clearly that our timetable is instant: food in five, supersize it please, then give me a quick fix to lose the pounds that that yummy supersized meal just created. We can be just a little cray-cray when you think about the yo-yo effect we create in our speedy lifestyles! Yet God's timing is filled with wisdom and discernment that is unfathomable to us, yet with hope that spans farer and wider than we would be able to see. Hope takes time and commitment. It is a delicate flower that needs constant care and attention. Bargaining gives our brain that time to wrap the concept of hope around our hearts. It is not only normal; it's needed. Hope serves a very important purpose. So this is why we will breathe slowly and steadily through this process. Let's be so careful not to beat ourselves up for those times when we thought, "OK, then I will stay here, and this will be my thorn" or "I will go one more day living this way." This is a process, a natural way for your body to say, "Hold up, I need to keep

Purposely Woven

trying. To keep seeing this situation as I need to see it." God will use all of this as we grieve. He will be patient as we brain bargain, then He will pull us out of that pit faster than we can say, "Help." He will rescue us to move forward into the reality of healing, into the next steps through which He will lovingly guide us.

Let's look at some verses to help us through this time as we face what God has placed before us in a time of deep disappointment and lost hope.

Write out Romans 15:13; _____

_____

_____

_____

_____

Vs.13 says God is the God of _____

_____

What are we to do? _____

_____

What do we get from that? _____

_____

By whose power? _____

_____

Purposely Woven

So, we have learned a chunk of goodness in this one Scripture! The Word is active and penetrating (Hebrews 4:12). It is filled with a wisdom that sits waiting to be opened and applied. What a gift! I get super excited when just one Scripture can impact so, so much once it's unlocked. God, who is the hope-filler, will fill each of us with joy and peace when we seek and choose to believe His word. But this is never done on our own or in our own power. We have a friend, a sidekick – the Holy Spirit! He is here and has the power to guide us. A willingness from us is all that's needed.

What holds you back from believing or being willing?

_____

_____

Write out Psalm 119:114: _____

_____

_____

Where do we place our hope? _____

_____

Who hides and shields us? _____

_____

What hopes do you need to place before God today? What do you need to lay before the Lord for Him to shield you this day, week, year?

Purposely Woven

_____

_____

_____

_____

Here's the deal. God is the only source of real hope. It's as simple as that! Yet we let lesser things get tangled into our tapestry when we choose to find hope in what the world offers. It's tricky, I know. It happens so slowly and simply and becomes this messy pile we never intended. We can place our hope in things that seem harmless or even good at first— people, church, relationships, material things, jobs, titles, etc.—but the truth is, those are just misplaced hope. They *will* disappoint. They *will* fail us! Even the most beautiful relationship can crumble and snag at the very fabric of your soul. When hope is properly placed in God and God alone, those snags will hurt – they will set us back, yes – but they will not break or define us. When we have hope properly placed, the circumstance, person, or accusation will not determine our worth. Hope in God will be the foundation of the truth on which we stand.

Purposely Woven

Use this space or grab your journal and write out a prayer to God. How will you begin to place your hope in him today?

Six

Untangling Darkness

The light shines in the darkness, and the darkness has not overcome it.
John 1:5

Feelings... just the word replays visions of how vividly they have orchestrated important roles in so many seasons of my life. Some of those seasons have brought a great harvest and some fields of decay. Feelings are there even when we don't call upon them. They are constant and real. Feelings can bring us to a place of so much joy and happiness that we can never think of ever being unhappy again. Then they can bring us so much heartbreak that we are literally peeling ourselves off the floor to start the next day. Feelings can be our best friend and our arch nemesis, sometimes all in the same day! We all have and need them. As we investigate this phase of grief, it is, oh, so important to remember to *feel* what you are feeling. Don't let others tell, bribe, or guilt you into feeling something you're not. If you are hurting, then face your hurt! If you are angry, then admit that anger. If we suppress our feelings and emotions, we do not acknowledge the pain. In doing so, we ignore the existence of the war raging inside of us. The reality of what IS there.

Now, this can be confusing to some of us. Some of us here have been taught not to live by our feelings but to overcome them. Let's clarify for a moment. When we are grieving, there is an uprooting of hurt that has brought these emotions to surface. It can come out as anger or bitterness or reclusiveness and distant behavior. We are not talking about minor disappointments. We are talking about great hurt that can give birth to emotions that fester and want to wriggle free from our body and minds. At this point, it is very important that we express the feeling that we are dealing with to a family member, friend, church family member, grief support counselor, etc. Another way to express our feelings when we are grieving is tapping into our creative side by journaling, painting, writing, etc. These exercises can help channel unhealthy feelings into prayers, art, and *maybe even a book* to help ourselves and others heal.

There is power in speaking truth and admitting feelings out loud. I know this to be so evident in my own journey of healing. Through my times of grief, I would feel certain emotions bubbling to the surface, ready to explode! It was when I got together with a godly friend or mentor and finally spoke that feeling, that I could face the reality of it. I was keeping it all locked up, dealing with it in my mind and heart, yet when it was said to another—said out loud—the power in that was freeing. There is something about audibly verbalizing our inside wrestling that can bring a clarity to situations. When we bring it to the surface, pulling it from the deep hole we were hiding it in, it gets a chance to breathe. Can I say, friends that it usually is much more manageable than what we *felt* it was? The real work is done when we are open, even if that honesty paints us in a light that does not give the glow, we thought we sore, or wanted to display. Sometimes this is with you and God (which I highly recommend), and sometimes this is with another living breathing soul whom you undoubtedly trust.

Often, with the expression of my feeling comes a relief and comfort in knowing that even after I confessed, my friends don't think I'm crazy! I said it, and they still want to be my friends! I have said some hard and honest stuff in my days. My family and true friends (God bless their lovely souls) have loved me and stuck by my side through some scary and confusing trials. Maybe they are just feeling sorry for this intense brown-eyed girl, staying my friends out of pity, but I don't really believe that. I know how honored I am by their commitment and investment. I pray it has and continues to be reciprocated through my actions to them as well.

Even more than time in community, my time with God, pouring out my innermost hurts and desires, is by far the most healing experience, time and time again! He has not walked away from this crazy girl! He will not abandon us because we choose to be honest with our deep feelings.

Purposely Woven

Openness is healing freedom. It releases the bondage in our minds and souls.

There are emotions we can learn to watch for as we weave through this darkness. There are different emotions that can surface, triggering another wave of unhealthy feelings that may spiral us right back into that hole of displaced truth. All can be going great... and then we find ourselves back on the kitchen floor in a puddle of deep pain, weeping while the sauce is boiling over on the stove. That is why it is so important that we are in God's Word first. That we bathe in the truths that He has spoken over each of us. Reading and journaling, daily in and out of trials through the book of Psalms. Is one of the most comforting, truth-seeking reality checks for me when I find myself wading in emotions that can leave me drowning in my own destructive thoughts. His Word sets me upright, silencing the lies I have created to trying to mask the feeling or emotion.

When emotions are triggered and we find ourselves in a depressive state, there is always a root, a cause. I am currently walking a season where a dear family member has chosen to distance themselves from me and my family. There is great confusion and hurt tossing the waves of this hurting heart, causing them to make those decisions. This rejection has brought on gut-twisting pain I never imagined possible and was not prepared for. There have been days of deep discomfort and loneliness, days I felt I was missing of one of the limbs from my very body. I have felt abandonment in the deepest form. Anxious thoughts swirl through my mind: "If this relationship fails or severs, then I have failed." Through deep pain, I have chosen to step back out of the fog the enemy likes to create around me in my weakness and seek to find the truth amidst the haze.

In this situation, I was able to see that the *root of my pain* was created from my own pride in my relationship with this person. You see, if I am not in this person's life and others see, then I am going to be perceived in various negative ways: people may think I don't love them or that I'm a neglectful person—or, worse, that *I* have abandoned *them*.

None of that is truth! Yet those thoughts about how I may be perceived caused a wave of fear to rise within me. So I learned to take untrue thoughts captive (2 Corinthians 10:5) and soak in the truth of who God says I am in His word. I know the *truth* about the choices I have made in this relationship. I know *truth* about what kind of investment has been poured into the relationship. The reality is, people will *always* have opinions and talk about your situations. You know the truth; you have walked each step of it.

What blinds you from the truth? Combat it with the Word. Speaking about what the *root to your pain* is to a trusted friend or family member also helps when those times come. These precious people can be your champions, helping you not to give in to the lies that the enemy wants to tangle in your tapestry, to muddy your colors. Let's look at some scriptures to help navigate through this stage of grief.

Write out Psalm 18:2-3: _____

_____

_____

Purposely Woven

In whom does this remind us to take refuge? _____

Verse 3 says, "I will _____ *upon the Lord."*

To call upon the Lord is to be in prayer with Him, to know Him intimately and to form a deeper relationship. I may say this a hundred more times before these pages end: prayer is our lifeline to relationship with God. We would not expect to have a fruitful, healthy marriage if we never talked to or spent time with our spouse, right? It's no different with God. In fact, it is abundantly more important! If I am praying and cultivating my relationship with God, then I am most likely thirsting for the Word more. If I am in the Word more, then I am craving my time with God, maybe even *coveting* that time. By this, I get to know not just *about*

Him, but I get to know *Him,* who He is, His character. We want to know Him more and more, right? We pray because He is worthy. But it does not end there; He is so much more generous than that. He always gives back way more than He gets. The last line of verse three says "I am saved from my enemies." You are saved; you are protected and redeemed through Him. Furthermore, the beauty of God's complete plan is that our character becomes more aligned with His. Our ideas of who we should be begin to shift. We will then have more fruitful, intimate relationships with those He places in our lives. The power of prayer is always at our disposal and never ceases to amaze!

All of this is to say, prayer is nonnegotiable. It will lift us when we are cemented to the floor, crippled by pain, or devastated by tragic news. Prayer will guide us when we are lost in feelings of deep doubt or discouragement. It will speak truth when the enemy has another agenda. When negativity wants to weave its putrid colors into our beautiful masterpiece, we have the option *and* the tools to reject them from displacing what the artist has planned for our tapestries through speaking Scripture and truth in prayer.

I will say, it does take commitment, friend. It is not for the faint of heart. Tenacity and dedication are your prayer partners. These two need to walk daily hand in hand in the midst of your prayer practices to accomplish what God intends through this fellowship with Him. I know you have the power in you to stick with it and start making your prayer life align with the dreams God has for you! God supplied us all with the same access to His grace and mercy every single second of the day. Some just look for it harder than others. I want to be one of those *earnest lookers,* don't you?

Use this space to call upon the Lord. Speak to the One who never disappoints. How will you this week, today start to become an earnest looker

Seven

Untangling Anger

"Be angry and do not sin; ponder in your own hearts on your beds and be silent." Psalm 4:4

"I am not angry, just a little frustrated": that has come out of my mouth more times than I would like to admit. But it's the truth. I have indulged in the same little lie that too many of us feed ourselves. We deny our anger, but I think we can all admit there has been a time or two that we all wanted to throw a good right hook in the general direction of whomever or whatever was majorly irritating us. Now, I hope we all know that we can't go around knocking people out whenever we dang well please. (Well... we *could*, but I don't think it would make us feel any better. Might get us locked up with three square meals, but that would only add to our issues!) Is there a healthy alternative? How do we handle this feeling of anger that knocks us around? Can anger be easily washed away like a chalk drawing on the sidewalk? Do we keep it locked up away in our soul? Or do we become a slave to it?

Once again there are choices to be made. We are free to choose one of the above options... or allow me to offer up an alternative. Ownership. Yes, friend, we can choose to own our anger! Embrace it in all its glory. Are you with me? I am envisioning you throwing this book hard against a wall right about now. Or maybe you even have a roaring fire that could use some kindling? Please know, I am not speaking of anything I have not braved myself. I humbly want to offer up a suggestion that you embrace the anger that rages inside. Confront the visions, names, circumstances that are circling your head like hungry vultures. Allow yourself a moment to scream into your pillow or throw some right and left air punches around. (Maybe make sure no one is watching, especially the neighbor, if you don't feel like explaining.)

I just witnessed one of my grown children practicing this exercise while working on a broken vehicle. When I walked into the garage and witnessed him throwing right and left hooks at an invisible target, I asked, "Did you find the problem." He stopped, looked at me, and said, "Yep, and it's going to be way more work than I thought" – with a grimace, I might add. He was frustrated at the problem he faced and the amount of work it would require, so he wisely took it upon himself to risk looking like a fool in the comfort of the forgiving garage. He owned that he was angry but knew he had to move forward with the diagnosis, to find a healthy solution to the frustrating issue.

Anger is an intense emotion that is commonly associated with – even an indication of – love. We judge those we love sometimes more intense and with more severity than we would a stranger. The deeper we love, the deeper we feel, the higher and more intense our expectations for that loved one seems to be. We have all at one point or another in our lives been in that situation – a parent wanting to see her child succeed, a sibling sick over witnessing his brother or sister participate in activity that is harmful. Or a child speaking truth to a friend to protect him – only to lose or damage that relationship. All the pleading, truth telling, reminding, and disciplining comes from a heartfelt desire for what's best for them. When we see loved ones' gifts and potential, we want nothing less than to see them rise to the highest height they could reach. When we love others, we want to protect them from what could harm them. As we interact and invest in people, we become part of their weaving, investing in their dreams, or our dreams for them right alongside.

When someone we love hurts or betrays us in any form, then chooses *not* to restore or heal that hurt, it can most assuredly be one of the most painful of seasons to endure. We can choose to face the reality of it head-on and take ownership. Or we can stuff it down into a place where it will entangle all the other pieces in the weaving process and create a knotted, tangled mess. This will only do more damage to our souls, affecting not only us but also those around us.

I would suggest finding one of "your people," someone fully trustworthy to hold you through this and at the same time brave enough to love you with accountability and honesty. Often, we do not speak of the anger brewing inside for fear of being judged. We should cultivate a safe place to share anger in a healthy way—not by being labeled as "negative," "over-emotional," or "crazy," but as someone experiencing a natural emotion that God wants us to face. He asks us to look it in the mirror and own it. This is possible to do with the help of our God as well as faithful family and friends. We get the idea that anger is a bad seed that should be eradicated, not dealt with, but in truth, the more we look in the mirror and can see our anger for what it is, the more healthily we can move through our grieving and come to healing.

Purposely Woven

There are injustices in the world that God wants us to stand up and fight for. *Righteous* anger fuels us to do just that. And sometimes that injustice hits close to home. When a dear loved one of mine came forward with allegations of abuse by family members, I was angered, to say the least! I felt not just angry but disgusted, betrayed, deceived. Some of that has not changed. I am still disgusted and would never trust anyone I loved around those individuals. Because of this, I have educated myself regarding childhood abuse and am still to this day learning how I can help fight the fight for those affected by its traumatic aftermath it can weave into their fabric. I strive to come alongside those organizations who are fighting that battle for the voiceless children and adults worldwide who have been subject to such unthinkable crimes. However, I do not hold tight to the anger that enraged me when I first heard of it, nor do I let bitterness swirl in my belly over it anymore. I had – for my sanity and the sake of my future relationships – to choose to let God take it and do the judging. My focus had to be taken off the offender and transfer that time and attention to the hurting. I first stood beside the abused and supported their stand for the truth, their needs and wants, being ultra-aware of the demons that were threatening to destroy them through this evil choice. The next choice was to create boundaries in order to prevent those individuals from entering into or hovering around my circle. Anger and bitterness can evolve into a disease that will rot one's soul. More times than not, we must forgive people who will *never* ask for forgiveness. This act is for the health and sanity of *our* souls, not theirs. Forgiveness gives the forgiver the freedom to say, "I release hate and anger and replace them with confidence in God, trusting that He will right every wrong and judge my enemies."

Purposely Woven

I encourage you to choose today *not* to let anger and bitterness saturate the colors of your tapestry. Start practicing those punches, girl, and let it out! Please know I am by no means acting as if this is a quick-fix "let-go-and-let-God-love-thine-enemies" prayer here. Quite the opposite! We are asking God to heal us from any anger that we have let habitat in our hearts and minds for far too long! We are seeking to unfasten the bonds of bitterness that have entangled us in a web that seems unescapable. We *are not* accepting evil, sinful behavior that others have inflicted upon us, or those we love. We are just choosing to grow. Letting the Artist weave our tapestries as He sees them. Oh, and He *does* see us *and* the wrongs that have been done to us! Let's let God deal with our enemies. Really, wouldn't we rather He do it anyway? He knows what He is doing. His track record of making beauty from ashes is flawless. He promises our enemies *will not* go unpunished! Just read the story of Sodom & Gomorrah in the bible. God is a God of justice my friend

As we look at verses on anger, let's process through each one. Take your time with this. Don't rush. This is a process that takes delicate care and practice to navigate. God is right here, guiding each of us through.

Write out Ephesians 4:26-27

Purposely Woven

Does God say never to be angry? _____

_____

What sins rise up in our anger? _____

How can letting anger in give the devil "opportunity"?

_____

_____

_____

Write out Psalm 37:8-10

90

On what concern of yours do you "wait for the Lord"? _____

_____

_____

Anger is a dangerous force. It can start wars, destroy families, and cripple future generations. The enemy wants IT to be your go-to companion in trying times. For every trial and heartache we endure, the enemy whispers in our ears to justify the anger that boils beneath. "Refrain" and "forsake" – that is what my Bible says to do with anger. Some translations also say, "Turn away." Refraining is to "stay away from an impulse." Forsake means to "quit, leave, abandon, give up or renounce." Whatever you're waiting for, the Bible states clearly what our plan of action should be – to take no part in letting anger take root.

As you do your journal time, work through what you're waiting on and what anger you may be holding onto in your waiting. He already knows, friend. Yet how healing it is to go through the motions as we act out in faith to speak and write it! Truth comes forth and God begins to bind up that wound as we release it to Him.

Eight

Threading Acceptance

Our greatest fear should not be of failure, but at succeeding at things in life that don't really matter.
Frances Chan

Acceptance is a journey, *not* a destination. It's a process through which we choose diligently to work, not a final outcome. It can be the process of learning to live with a new normal. It might be coping with the death of a loved one. Coming to terms with a station in life that seems unfair or a relationship not mended to our liking or timetable. Maybe it's an abandonment you have experienced. It could be an illness that has trespassed into your life, threatening to take your future away. All these unexpected and fearful scenarios bring us to a crossroads. Do we see paths filled with choices to navigate through this time or dead ends halting us to a stopping point with nowhere to turn? For a period, you may feel like you have overcome and mastered the art of accepting your new situation. Then months or years later you may feel you're moving backwards. Be patient with yourself, extra careful not to rush through this. God will heal you step by step, slowly. He will weave just the right people, opportunities and situations in and out of your life at just the right moments to aid you in this healing process.

I can attest to times of thinking, "Great! I am on a roll here! My late-night pillow soaking episodes, unexpected shower meltdowns, air punching, pillow screaming days are long gone. I am feeling quite healthy and happy." Then maybe the holidays would come around – they do every year at the same time – and I would be so surprised by the feelings and emotions that would surge out of nowhere. I would fight the annoying thoughts: "Come on, Chiquita! We already took care of this. You don't have time for this again!" Can I encourage you to let it be what it needs to be *when* it needs to be? Lean into it; pay attention to where you are and what you are feeling. Pain does not just go away. In my experience, it only takes on another form in your day-to-day life, if not given a chance to breathe. I learned to embrace the pain of abandonment for what it was. I couldn't change the people who chose to leave me, but I *could* choose not to let it define me or who I would become. I would *not* forget the hurt it caused. I *would* use the remembrance of it to vow to *never* treat another human in that manner. I pray the pain I encounter from others can transform me into the likeness of Christ, not disfigure me it's with battle scars. Our wounds on the battlefield can be used mightily for ourselves and others to find victory and live with perspective, when we openly expose our wounds through this healing of accepting what is, NOT in what we want.

Sometimes I can laugh in the face of it, roll up my sleeves and say, "OK, let's do this." Feelings and thoughts of unworthiness, frustration, and of not being heard creep up—sometimes for me that can be all in one day. Sometimes, I am tempted to go back to my old ways of: "Come on, not now... ain't nobody got time for this!" When those days come, I must remind myself quietly and honestly to lean in and face the beast for what it is. It is amazing to me that the more I strive to die to self and become more like Christ, the more every encounter with my pain becomes more easily recognizable and manageable. These encounters are reduced to inconveniences. I quickly see them as paths to becoming closer to my Savior, drawing me further from the lies the world spews at me. Please don't misunderstand me. Life after great loss and grief does not return to "normal." What is that anyway? There is no *normal* to begin with, no standard, except God's for which we are to aim. As we accept where we are, we – little by little – embrace God's plan and purpose through the brokenness we experience. We are able with clearer vision to find what God is asking us to seek after, which is the beautiful story He chooses to weave in and through us, our *life*, and our tapestry! I pray you can use some of the encouragements below to manage times that may creep up on you as they do me:

Purposely Woven

1. Be in the Word daily! When I am armed with the Word, I am better able to tackle what the world throws at me in that day. Reading and praying through the Psalms is always a good place to go when I feel trapped, negativities greatest weapon.

2. Carve out a time—even if its 10 minutes every day—just to be still before God. Hear Him speak truth to you. Just be still and listen. This can be uncomfortable and seem like a waste of time at first if you are not familiar with this practice, but believe me, friend: it is a game changer! The Creator longs to spend time speaking into your soul. I promise, you won't be disappointed. Those 10 minutes will gradually become 30. Don't be surprised if you find yourself craving it!

3. Start a healing journal to track your journey through each of these stages. Write in it. Draw in it. *Yell* in it. This is a safe place for you to journal through the Psalms, writing them out, praying over them. Write your fears and hurts.

4. Start letting labels go! This is a journey I am on to this day. We are labeled in all areas, and sometimes we don't even realize it. Our family birth order, our siblings' comments, parents' nicknames for us, spoken condemnation over us, coworkers' views of us—releasing ourselves from these labels is so important in finding God's "normal" for you. I have found that this journey is as freeing

Purposely Woven

as we let it be. Start each day to be only who *HE* says you are! Hint... its right there in the Word!

Find 1 scripture that you can write out and come back to when negativity & discontentment creep up. Write it here!

Nine

Threading Release

Trials teach us what we are:
They dig up the soil and let us see what we are made of. Charles Spurgeon

Investment in something or someone requires sacrifice, choices, and giving of self. You see, doing the right thing is always the harder thing! Always! We live in days where mudslinging is a pastime, where believing and repeating lies is acceptable, and sin is embraced as a welcomed friend at the dinner table. There are a select few left standing alone. This can be one of the most hurtful, soul-damaging times in a person's life. It can literally be the breaking point for most individuals enduring it. Living through deep, heart shattering loss has taken many of us down very dark, lonely roads.

I have chosen to call out sin as God's Word calls us to many times. I have also found out standing up for this truth is not popular. It does not seem to make you many friends and in my experience seems to be an open invitation for judgment. It catches the masses by complete surprise and causes a wave of panic and fear! I lost childhood friends, family members who were dear to me, and a church family that I faithfully served alongside for over a decade. I was not prepared for the lack of concern that people seemed to have for God's truth. The fear of man was like a heavy, suffocating blanket under which people slumbered. I was shocked – the firsthand experience of witnessing those who would walk beside me on the clean and tidy road were the first to dart the other direction when things got messy. True character reveals itself when there is sin laid out on the table. When things get real, many people's M.O. is to tuck tail and run, leaving you alone with only muddy footprints left behind. This becomes our tangled realities, that require tending, not ignorance of its existence.

I remember the day when I was crying out to God, "Why?! Why would these people who claimed they loved me and my family just believe lies and choose to 'stay out of it'? Choose to abandon lifelong relationships? Didn't they care for me?" Then I heard God say, "Kele, people care more what other people think than what my Word says. Loving well requires seeking truth; seeking truth equals inconvenience and self-sacrifice." Acts 5:29 says, "We must obey God rather than men." This is the Scripture He spoke to me. I know it might sound simplistic to you, but to me it was a game-changer. I decided to take the challenge right then and there to learn to see God's truth and to accept whatever consequences came with that truth. Those around me were not ready yet. They were not willing to seek truth no matter the cost, and it was too inconvenient to love me in the dark spaces. I left that time with God clothed with a changed heart and attitude. It was time to stop fretting and thinking about what others thought or what truth they were willing or not willing to see. I knew the truth I lived, decades that no one else experienced. In the home *I* cultivated and nested. Where *I* grew as a woman, as a mother. Where *I* loved fiercely and ached in secret spaces. Where *I* learned how to become what God called me to be. Also, where *I* fought to save what was built.

As I started that journey of truth, I became more focused on what God was speaking into me—the where, what, and why of my part in this story. I would own what I was responsible for, every part I may have played in hurting or sinning against another. What I was not willing to own, though, was that which others had placed upon me. Accusations spewed at me were never mine to claim or carry. This journey took longer than I thought. Just when I thought I had it figured out, had it all buttoned up, I would hear another lie or comment about myself and how outsiders perceived the situation. I found myself asking, "Am I what they say I am? Do I deserve the sin others have committed against me?" I would wrestle with what the world screamed at me for a bit, and then I would get back on that narrow road and remind myself where my focus and truth must be to take ownership of only what God has asked me to acknowledge. I let the rest fall like dead leaves to the ground and be swept away by the wind. I came to the freeing conclusion that at the end of each day, I answer to Him and only Him. He is my only judge. If I have wronged anyone according to this lens and truth, He will convict my heart to repent and restore that matter. If we are willing to commit to this kind of soul searching, He will reveal all wrongs within us that need righting. 1 Chronicles 28:9 says God searches and understands a person's whole heart. If we are searching, He will reveal what He sees as sin and purge it from us. 1 Chronicles 29:17 says, "God tests the heart and has pleasure in uprightness of the heart." This is where we start—opening it all to God, letting the One who knows *both* sides of every story reshape and refine where He sees fit to do so. He knows our hearts, our struggles, and our fights.

This season was a difficult pruning for my soul. It also taught me many imperative lessons. One of those lessons was *never* to assume you know what goes on behind the walls of someone's home. Sin can put on a lovely dress, sport a very handsome smile. It presents itself as the clean-cut, all-American, trustworthy citizen. Seeing past the beautiful layers it creates is exhausting. I sadly experienced this in a front row, center seat, eating the biggest bowl of popcorn you ever saw! I am sure if we were sitting together, we could each take turns telling heartbreaking stories of the lies and sin that were masked in our lives. Crafted so expertly that others were permanently blinded by their beauty—even while you were screaming at the top of your lungs for help to be freed from it. The point here is, there will always be those who choose not to see sin for what it is. Even though it goes against every fiber in you to walk away from finding vindication, I am encouraging you to let God fight this fight for you. It's time for you to own what you know as truth and release everything else.

Purposely Woven

Choose to place truth over your wound then lay your burden on the altar for God to heal.

Proverbs 23:26 says, "My son [my daughter], give me your heart, and let your eyes observe my ways." He's calling us to pay attention, to turn our eyes and ears to Him and what He wants for us. James 4:6-7 tells us, "God opposes the proud but gives grace to the humble. Submit yourselves therefore to God. Resist the devil and he will flee from you." To submit requires a willing act, an acceptance of God's authority. This means we believe that He has ultimate power and guidance over every situation, over every hurt we have felt, over every lie spoken. He rectifies every sin committed against us. He knows our hearts intimately. When we are willing to lay our burdens on that altar of His redemptive grace, He will take every single one. We will see them no more. We are washed clean and ready to move forward, seeking His wisdom for the future. We are also advised in this verse to resist the devil. Satan is powerful but *not* invincible! When we choose to place on the armor of God (Ephesians 6:10-17), evil will flee from us. The devil will move right along to the next victim.

I pray we are each so saturated in the Word, aware of our own temptations and shortcomings, that we are the first to admit our faults and sins. In doing so, we focus less on the faults of others. Let's meditate through a couple of questions to help guide us on this journey.

In your journal or in the space below, ask God to search your heart and reveal what/whom you need to release to Him today.

Purposely Woven

Is there a certain area that you feel Satan keeps knocking you down and/or tempting you?

_____

_____

_____

_____

_____

Where are you feeling depleted? Is there a place in the Word that you can go to for advice and counsel on this?

_____

_____

_____

_____

In Colossians 3, we are told what to stay away from and to "put on the new self, being renewed in knowledge after the image of the creator" (vs. 10). Friend, I want to encourage you to keep your heart and mind focused on just that–knowing your Creator so intimately that you are renewed by it. As you own who you are and where you have been, lift your head high and walk with confidence into the days ahead. As we close this chapter, turn your Bible to Psalm 51. I know it may take time, but I urge you to first read it and then write it out–yes, all of it–word for word. This chapter has been my go-to when I need to speak with God, to be cleansed and reminded that "[He delights] in the truth in the inward being, and [He teaches] me wisdom in the secret heart" (vs.6). Let God do His job of renewing a right spirit within you today!

Purposely Woven

Ten

Method of Mending

"But the LORD is faithful, he will establish you and guard you against the evil one." 2 Thessalonians 3:3

"The Lord is near to the brokenhearted and saves the crushed in spirit" (Psalm 34:18). He is near to us in our loss, abandonment, brokenness, pain, heartbreak, and confusion. What do we do, then, when we feel alone, broken into so many pieces that we are questioning if repair is possible? We choose to mend, and then we act. Your brain might possibly be spinning: "Really, Kele, you have no idea. I have been trying to heal, to forget, to forgive and move forward with [fill in the blank]." I don't want to minimize or try to say that I understand your pain. I am positive your [fill in the blank] is so raw and real to you that my attempt to understand would be futile. This mending process is difficult, gritty, and honestly can look ugly at times. It takes brutal honesty, first from and about oneself and often from and about others. It takes days from our months, hours from our days, and minutes from those hours. The pain is so real that it cannot at times be expressed into words. It's like the ripping apart of your very heart.

This, sadly, is a feeling I have lived through on more than one occasion. There was a season when someone close to my heart chose to walk away from truth, from reality. This path took him to the front door of lies and the deceit the enemy offered. I felt broken, betrayed. I experienced a physical pain in my body that was unexplainable. I ached and wept with deep groaning's.

Then I braved the season of walking someone dear to me through a dark journey as they exposed a truth to me of years silently suffering as a child through abuse. Of how they navigated living in survival mode for decades behind a mask of self-preservation. I ached with the need to shoulder the aftermath of 'self-blame that abuse placed upon them. Their struggles of what if's, and self-shaming, made me physically ill from hearing this horrific act committed against this precious person. How does one move forward? How do we choose to forgive and not to hate? For that to occur, pain must be tended and mended. Like tending a garden, pain like this needs deep, soil-turning, hands-black-with-the-mud-of-the-earth toiling.

You, dear sister, most likely have had a deep ache, or maybe not one but *many*. I am sure each one of them could use some tending and mending. The beauty in God's love for us and mercy upon us is that He gently guides us through the mending. We have a choice – to seek wisdom and guidance on how to mend or choose to let that hurt rot inside of us. Choosing the latter will make us bitter, threatening to swallow us in its pit of ugly despair.

As I walked that precious soul through healing from abuse, I remember a turning-point discussion we were able to have. There was great strength in bringing truth to light which ultimately led to slow and steady healing. Ironically, the more honest they were, the more difficult the healing seemed to become. Every couple of weeks I would witness a great wall come up around them, closing in the pain. The need to grieve and desire to heal were engaged in tug-of-war with desires to be, or to appear, "normal." This truth revealed would forever change the dynamics of all that was to come; they would be different because of it. This change was unwelcomed and brought up a righteous anger. As our discussion became real, I saw the struggle intensifying—to dive into what was comfortable and safe or to run head-on into the truth. We were at a crossroads. These conversations are difficult! Because these choices are difficult!

When it's time to stand up and choose, we are either going to trust God in His timing according to His ways, or we are going to choose to do it our way. I think many times for believers our default response is, "Of course, I choose God's path." Really, though, it is not "of course." The choice is yours. Requiring action, not head knowledge, which will determine the future course of your journey. Everyday choices add up to the big decisions we weave into our lives. Quite simply, we are going to choose God's way or the world's. We are either going to move forward or stay stuck in the tangled web made up of grievous sin and lies. I have been at this crossroad more than once. I also venture to say you, my friend, are either there right this very second, have been there, or will be. The choice to brave the path of trusting God with your most tender hurts and secrets can be one of the most difficult decisions to make. Time will stop, and days will move more slowly at times. It can be exhausting. Doubt, a need for validation, and embarrassment nag at us in those days. When others around us witness us taking the sticky step into self-searching and the cleaning out of past wounds, it can look unnatural to them. The world tends to leave well enough alone, sweeping pain and hurt under the rug. Working through pain is inconvenient, and most people want things to stay nice and tidy. However, trusting God brings unexplainable joy, unshakable truth, ultimate healing, security, and safety. It is a harder, longer road that will reward us for eternity! The road the world races along is filled with self-satisfaction, temporal fun, popularity, feeling good, and instant gratification. That is why it is so crowded, my friend. It satisfies for a time but only lasts for a brief blink. Then those familiar feelings of confusion, pain, and doubt creep right back in. The path to mend is hard. It is a foreign road to most, not heavily traveled. It is only reserved for the brave and courageous, not for the weak.

Scripture guides us in this mending process. Romans 15:13: "May the God of hope fill you with all joy and peace in believing so that in the power of the Holy Spirit, you may abound in hope." Allow yourself time, time to be filled with joy and peace. This will happen only when you choose to step up to say, "I am broken, and I need your hope, your joy, your peace." He is waiting to fill those empty spaces with those promised gifts. Isaiah 40:31: "They who wait for the Lord shall renew their strength; they shall mount up on wings like eagles; they shall run and not be weary; they shall walk and not be faint." *Mount, run, walk*: these verbs are the vivid colors and moments in our tapestries, depicting a life of faith. We are to be strengthening our faith, active in the fight, transforming our character. This is one of my life verses, and I say it over and over, applying it year after year, season after season. It speaks might and truth over every bit of my life, no matter what age or stage. Are you able to take a breath, to step back and wait? We are asked to choose, to wait, to let Him renew our strength and then to run towards His word, His timing, and His plan and purpose. This will look different for us all. Part of the beauty and sustainability in mending is the waiting. This is so foreign to our society and culture. Waiting is an intentional daily practice; waiting is a choice we make deliberately that strengthens our character. Your wait and my wait are as unique as our fingerprints. The length of it and how it comes to fruition will depend on many factors, and it is unique experience for each individual. Where and why it will take place is reserved especially for you, my friend.

If I could humbly offer up some advice on this wait journey... try to be extra careful about how and of whom you seek advice during this mending period. Well-meaning friends and family members are eager to give advice. They, of course, love you and don't want to see any more pain in your life. They want you to heal. My experience has taught me to be careful to whom I "vent" during this tender time. I learned to be wise about revealing my pain to any listening ear. Having a Biblical mentor is so very important. There was a time in my life that I had to pray for God to bring me one (or two). Once you have her, speak your hurt to her. I also learned (the hard way) to pray over my circumstances far more than I talked or vented about them. This sounds so simple, yet it was a struggle for me. I had plenty who wanted to grumble with me over the injustices done to me. Yet I needed to rein in that monster and learn that nothing good comes from recounting wrongs. I needed to sink deep into prayer with the right people covering it all. God's timing is *so* not our timing. His plan is vastly different than what we imagine. The sooner I took that truth captive and made it part of my being, my eyes were opened to the reality that I have *no clue*! I am completely in service to Christ, and all will happen in a time, place, and reason upon that realm. I am *free*! Free to wait, trust, mend, and let God be God, allowing Him to speak strength and purpose into my very soul. What a gift this time of mending can be if we are open to letting it breathe fresh insight into us!

Lamentations 3:22-23 says, "The steadfast love of the Lord never ceases; his mercies never come to an end; they are new every morning; great is your faithfulness." God's mercy, which is a covenant devotion to us, unending in His compassion, will *never* run out. He is faithful and will see to our mending personally and with acute attention! Friends, please latch onto this gem. Take this and hide it in your most treasured spot. As you mend, you will need to believe this truth without any doubt. He is there: He has a purpose to your mending and a plan for your tomorrow. Meditate on that truth and these verses:

Write out Isaiah 40:31:

What are two things that you have waited on the Lord for that He has fulfilled in your life?

Purposely Woven

_____

_____

_____

What are two things that make you weary and faint right now in your life? Can you give them to God and ask Him to take them from you without turning around and picking them right back up? Can you trust Him with them?

_____

_____

_____

_____

Write out Lamentations 3:22-23: _____

_____

_____

_____

How has God showed you steadfast love through either your current trial or a past trial?

_____

_____

_____

_____

Purposely Woven

Do you believe that God's mercies are new every morning? When we are grateful, our mind and attitude change. Write out a prayer to Him today thanking Him for His mercy and faithfulness you see in your life today, this week.

Eleven

Method of Binding

"Fear not for I am with you; be not dismayed for I am your God; I will strengthen you; I will help you; I will uphold you with my righteous right hand."
Isaiah 41:10.

Psalm 147:3: "He heals the brokenhearted and binds up their wounds." To bind means "to encircle, fasten around, to secure." I say, yes please! I would like to secure and fasten up some wounds! How about you? If we believe His word to be true, it says right here that He will "bind up" our every wound. Once again, this process may not be the drive-through, quick-fix, daily delivery to which we are accustomed. This is in God's timing, not ours. While raising my littles, whenever there was a conflict or issue, my kids were taught to say they were sorry if they offended each other, and the other was expected to say, "I forgive you." I look back now and think about how many times, I am sure, they each walked away, and their little 3rd-grade brains were like, "Um... I really didn't like that (----) he said, did etc. about me, and it really hurt." They instead, pasted a smile on to move forward. Why? Because we are taught not to hold grudges that moving forward and forgetting makes everyone happy, and happy people will never hurt again, right? Oh, I wish that to be the truth friends!

We first need to know what our wounds *are* in order to move forward in binding/fastening them. Then we must take each offense, feeling, and hurt and release them forever—throwing them into the flowing river of freedom and watching them wash swiftly down the riverbed of redemption! When we let God go about binding up our wounds, we are vacating spaces in our souls, spaces that were once overcrowded with lists of labels, pockets of pain, and hidden crevices of shame and regret. We can now fill those spaces with joy, acceptance, and truth spoken over us by our Maker. We can choose never to let ourselves or another person have the permission to speak shame upon us again. By doing so, each hidden crevice of pain begins to close, day after day, as God's healing word balm bind the wounds. One day revealing a tiny scar that is evidence of living and surviving a great and mighty battle. What a beautiful picture that paints for you and me! I am sitting here envisioning faces I have never seen and will most likely never meet; yet I know you are there, you are real, and you are fighting! So, what I see is beauty.

One way God binds our wounds is through deep and healthy friendships. Find others who will encourage you to seek truth, embrace joy, and say goodbye to old wounds. Proverbs 27:6a says, "Faithful are the wounds of a friend." When friends have our best interest in mind, they may speak truth into our lives that hurts. But they will stand beside us when we are at our ugliest and darkest. I remember my children going through dark times in their teenage years. It seemed the more a stand was taken for spiritual and moral behavior, the further they were pushed out of the popular social circles. I remember having one of those "car talks." (Those are the best, aren't they, moms? When you have them strapped in like little prisoners, captive to your every word!) This car talk was centered on how lonely this season was for them. How easy it would be to just bend to what was popular to gain friendships and popularity back. How hurtful the condemning looks from his peers felt. How experiencing abandonment really hurt. I tried to gently remind these soon-to-be-adults of mine (as I was also speaking to myself) the truth that true friends will be the ones standing there when we are no fun. When we are at our weakest and difficult to love. Having one or two true friends is far better than being in the "it" group of twenty. The twenty may make us feel important, even wanted, but will they be there when life gets difficult?

I encourage you to be thankful for the one or two, those tried and true, stick-with-you-through-the-blue, sisters. Be wise and mindful to find your tribe. My tribe is tiny, and, girl, I *love* it that way! They have seen me ugly cry, and I mean the kind of ugly that scares even me. They have pulled

Purposely Woven

me out of pits that I would willingly just sink right into and die. They have laid hands and prayed over me. We are given the gift of other believers to help us do this binding – to live, breathe, cry, pray, and at times slap each other into reality – as we allow God's promises to encircle our loss, grief, brokenness, and heartache.

2 Samuel 22:20 says, "He brought me out into a broad place, he rescued me because he delighted in me." Yes, God *delights* in you. He desires to rescue you from your brokenness and fasten it with the truth of His Word. James 4:8 says, "Draw near to God, and He will draw near to you." He does what He says He will do! He will never disappoint. His Word can always be trusted. We can rest in the security that He will be our fortress. Rest assured, allowing Him to bind our wounds will bring us a peace of mind and sense of safety we have never felt before. Psalm 46 states

some bold things: we should not fear even if all around us is giving way; since God is within us, we are to not be moved; and the God of Jacob is our fortress.

Please read through and write out all of Psalm 46. It is so powerful and filled with words of strength for our souls. He is with us, and He is our fortress! Amen to that! We can cast out all our fears, insecurities, and past brokenness upon those broad shoulders. We can pour out ourselves and be filled with Him, binding up the pain that we have held so tightly to and giving it to Him, friend, letting Him throw it into the deepest hole to never resurface again.

Write out Psalm 46. Highlight the verses that speak to you today.

Twelve

Intertwine Healing

"For I will restore health to you, and your wounds I will heal, declares the Lord."
Jeremiah 30:17

Once our wounds are mended and bound, God creates space for deep healing. Without the ability to heal, we would be perpetually broken and damaged beyond repair. Healing does not mean the damage never existed. It just means that damage no longer controls us. If healing were not possible, then hope would be nonexistent, all of God's promises lies, and God Himself unable to be trusted. But healing *is* possible, and I can speak from experience that He is trustworthy, friend! His healing is a gift, a treasure. Healing can be difficult and at times all-consuming. Honesty is required, and forgiveness is imperative. Sometimes this forgiveness is for things for which we need to forgive ourselves. Sometimes it is for something that was done to us or against us.

God's definition of forgiveness is so easily misinterpreted. I pray that for each area in which you are needing to impart forgiveness, you know without a doubt, you are not *forgetting* by *forgiving*. You are choosing to replace the hurt, anger, and possibly shame with wisdom and grace, but by no means do you justify the behavior. Letting go of negativity is necessary for healing, and by letting go, you move above and beyond what weighs you down. From letting go comes forgiveness, from forgiveness healing, and from healing freedom – the freedom to dream, to plan, and to

Purposely Woven

live in the potential God intended for your life. This makes healing a vessel to wholeness. Satan wants nothing more than to see us slaves to pain and confusion. If he can keep us in a whirlpool of hurt and bitterness, then he has us right where he wants us. We are useless when we camp on the mountain of the broken and bruised. Healing gives birth to confidence! It shows just who you were in your brokenness and opens your eyes to what you can and will become once you are set free from those chains. Brokenness brings with it lessons and through those lessons wisdom that we would have never known before. It is from where we are broken that we draw our strength. When we choose to heal, we gain power slowly. Healing is not a race but a daily commitment to choose to allow God to weave His truth and grace into our tapestry. Day after day, confidence becomes a companion.

Read Psalm 34, paying close attention to verses 8-15.

What does verse 14 say are we to turn away from? _____

_____

What are we to do? _____

_____

What are we to seek and pursue? _____

_____

Purposely Woven

This passage reminds us that the eyes of the Lord are on the righteous. His ears are open to our prayers. The creator of the universe just spoke and said to each of us that his eyes and ears are on us, girls! He attentively watches us, lovingly guides us along the path, when we choose to follow His call and live in His will. His ears are open to hear our prayers, waiting to hear what we are asking in His name! That gets me pumped! He cares and wants to hear from you and me. That is all we need, right? Drop mic and exit stage left! He will and does fight our battles for us. We just need to be obedient. I know, you're thinking, *"Just* obedience, huh?" Obedience is as tough as we make it. It is based on trusting His plan, not our own, trusting He has perfect timing in the who, what, and when of our lives. Forgiveness is so essential in healing, and it is all about obedience. Forgiveness is far more about you and what God is asking of your obedience than it is about the person you are called to forgive. I believe this fiercely because I have lived it. I have walked the road of having to forgive what was ugly, vile, and by the world's standards unforgivable. God stepped in, held my hand, bound up the wounds, and guided me toward the freedom of forgiveness and into a beautiful life. I pray you choose to walk that path, too, my friend. I can promise that you will never regret breaking the chains that entangle your wounds. Freedom in forgiveness is yours. Be open to it and watch miracles in your soul happen.

Write out a prayer to God asking Him to take your hand and guide you along those first steps toward forgiveness... and healing.

Thirteen

Weaving Restoration

The question is not what we intended ourselves to be, but what He intended us to be when He made us. He is the inventor, we are only the machine. He is the painter, we are only the picture.
CS Lewis

By the time we come out of the deep valley and step into the sunlight, we have grieved loss, owned our part, mended from the brokenness, allowed God to bind up the hurt, chosen healing through forgiveness, and we are... tired! It takes a toll on the mind and body to accomplish such important, life-breathing tasks. The valley has taught us to take stock of where we are and where we have been, to spend the time needed there, and then start the journey home. We are privileged if we choose to see the beauty in being broken before God and the freedom that flows from it. Allowing Him to be in control of our brokenness can and will create wide spaces for healing. This battle will become a memory of sacrifices made for a purposeful future. Birthing a unique beauty that has the potential to shine brighter than we imagined while fighting its war.

1 Peter 5:10-11 tells us clearly and confidently just what we can gain from suffering through the deep valleys: "And after you have suffered a little while, the God of all grace, who has called you to His eternal glory in Christ, will himself restore, confirm, strengthen, and establish you. To Him be the dominion forever and ever Amen." What a beautiful promise to hear

and know to be true! There is a whole lot packed into these verses. Grab a cup of your favorite stuff, then let's spend some time here unpacking this gift. "Suffered a little while": this first verse could be sending some of us out there into a little bit of a tizzy. You may be biting back the words, "*Little while, my foot!*" Some of us have been broken and suffered for years. Let's remember, ladies that God has a timetable we cannot even begin to comprehend. I stopped a long time ago trying to understand why it's not all happening as quickly, or in some cases as slowly, as I want it to. We are asked to trust Him and to know He has a plan we just can't even begin to understand. Can we choose to see the beauty in being able to sit back and let Him be God? When that concept really starts to seep in, we live, make decisions and speak so much differently. Let us not let our timelines and our lack of understanding get us all caught up before the next phrase: "the

God of all grace." In His grace, God bestows help and enough strength for each trial. His eternal plan for all believers is to bring them to glory. When we are in Christ, God bestows that grace upon us in this life and the life to come. It is His blessing to us! The Word says that "Christ himself will restore, confirm, strengthen and establish you." Ok, I don't know if that gets you excited, but it gets me really pumped! This God who created the very dirt I walk on, the dirt from which He created Man – this God wants to restore me ("to bring [me] back to a former, original, to a state of health, soundness or vigor")! Well, my goodness, where can I click on JOIN? I want me some bringing back, adding in some soundness of mind, body, and vigor! We all would sign up to put some life back into our bones, I am sure.

Purposely Woven

God tells us He Himself will do this. He is willing, and so must we be. We must choose to saturate ourselves with the Word, to be so filled with truth that each attempt to let a lie seep in will be rejected promptly by truth we have embedded into our minds and hearts. That is where your soundness will come in. You will look different, feel more alive, have passion to wake up each day with a joy that cannot be explained or dictated by circumstances. I have had dark days with extreme heartbreak – and I still do as I type these words. There are stressful situations and broken relationships that are lost in the world's evil. Yet *I* am not confused. *I* am not broken. I have a joy that radiates through my bones. It's real and cannot be taken away without my permission. You, my friend, have the ability to this as well. You are whole, not broken; you dwell in truth, not confusion.

Let us not let what enters our lives from the outside dictate joy that comes from within us. You have that joy in you! You do!

Once you tap into that reality, the process of attaining that joy will be evident. All points to Christ, His grace, and the eternal glory to which He has called you. He will confirm in each of us what the purpose was behind the pain, trial, heartbreak, and lack of understanding. This confirmation will bring us to a place where we are more aware of who we are, of the path we just emerged from, and of those around us. Often there is a need for repentance once the unknown is made known. Your path to restoration is yours to celebrate, needing no other validation. What freedom that brings to our core!

To confirm something is to establish a truth. To validate it. Giving it a genuineness that no one can debate. It is beautiful, and it's yours! I can testify to that sweet time of coming out of a valley and being changed, sometimes in big ways and sometimes with tiny sparks that catch fire in my heart. I have been challenged to be more compassionate to those around me. My responses have changed to situations that before would have brought forth a judgmental response. The next verse says, "He says He will strengthen us." He will mentally and spiritually make you stronger. You will have the power from your creator to say, "I am able." You are able to climb over that wall of depression, out of that valley of disappointment, across the desert of unknowing, and above the abyss of regret. Why? Because He has instilled in you grace that is sufficient for every single occasion.

In every unexpected need that meets you face-to-face, you have the gift of His strength. The greatest part is, you need do nothing but trust Him.

This *trust* thing is very hard for most of us to grasp. I know I lived in I-got-this-ville for quite a while. I really thought I had released control and trusted Him completely with my family, specifically with my children. It was not until the foundation of my I-got-this world was sinking like fine sand under my feet that I really did get it! I am only strong when I am weak. This is so foreign to us, yet so very true. He wants to be what you and I can't be for ourselves. Can we let Him? Can we release that need to have it all taken care of? The want to have and know all the answers? Are we willing to jump into the freedom of His strong arms? Trust the One who promises to provide a strength we could have never imagined?

Through that strength He establishes us. Establish: "To install or settle into position. To build. To show to be valid or true. To be accepted or recognized." This is what Mr. Webster says this means, so right about now, he is my BFF! I love how in 1 Peter 5:10, God uses the word *strengthen* right before *establish*. When we have endured trials and make it through the processes of grieving and healing, we find ourselves in a time of restoration. There is a settling in, a new installation happening in our hearts. The past is not forgotten but woven into our tapestry. It does not define; it refines. It strengthens our hearts and souls, then establishes within us a truth that we live with passion and purpose.

With fresh new hearts brimming with passion, purpose, and wisdom, we are now in position to move purposefully ahead. Instead of being in survival mode, we breathe purpose into each new day. Restoration becomes our blueprint for the building of this new life! How exciting this is! We can use any material we choose because we have the Master Builder at our side with super-power strength. We will rebuild on firmer shores, fashioning with wisdom, and stocking our tool bags with the knowledge of His Word and grace that comes from knowing we are cherished no matter what our circumstances are. No matter what the world says or sees us as, we know who we were created to be and what we were called to accomplish, and we know with all certainty that *no one* can steal, destroy, or take from us what is ours. We are here for "such a time as this." God does not make mistakes and wants to use every one of us mightily. We are filled with worth and purpose. We are not judging ourselves or circumstances on what is merely seen from the outside. We are wiser now with the depth and complexity of experience. We know that we are so much more than what some may choose to see and believe, and we remember that at the end of each day, we know Truth.

Purposely Woven

We will no longer live in the lies the enemy attempts to speak into our minds. He has the same tired tricks up his sleeve, and, quite frankly, I am unimpressed with his tactics! We can now remind ourselves that we are recognized and accepted by the only One who really matters. He knows our hearts and our motives. Remember this when you struggle or have hard days: we can rest in the shady hammock of peace, knowing we never again have to prove ourselves. We are sinners who have chosen to kick lies, hurt, loss, brokenness, and bad decisions in the teeth. We say, "So long, suckers! You no longer define me." By doing this, we give God the dominion over our lives forever and ever!

This, my friend, is your beautiful woven piece of tapestry. He continues to weave it for you. What material will you give to Him to use? The image of your beautiful tapestry hanging right next to mine brings chills to my arms and a lump in my throat. Just think, we are all interweaving, living out stories, walking paths that one day will intersect, comprising the grand tapestry story God has woven. One day we will be standing there looking at our masterpieces, tracing paths and valleys where we joined colors and never even knew it, where we brushed right past each other at times, lifting each other up unknowingly! I want to stand next to you, friend, and see your colors. We will weep happy tears together over trials overcome and hearts restored.

How has God restored you? If you feel you have not had a story of restoration yet, for what are you seeking restoration?

_____

_____

Purposely Woven

_____

_____

_____

Has God confirmed anything in you about a past or current trial?

_____

_____

_____

What are needing strength for today?

_____

_____

_____

_____

What is one thing you can do today to allow God to "establish" you today?

_____

_____

_____

_____

_____

Closing

You're Weaving

We have walked through some super heavy, life-altering, heart-searching chapters. We have learned that grief does not have to be our enemy; we don't have to let it get tangled up in our tapestry. We have the wisdom to know it can be just the friend we need to help us become who God calls us to be. It's our choice. Then, we walked through the process of owning and releasing what was entangling us, learning that truth needs to be spoken into the innermost hollows of our pain. Along the journey, we are learning that though this process may hurt, and it will (done to diligence) not be easy, yet there is beauty in the ownership of it. Only we can complete the task for ourselves: no one has the privilege or authority to do it for us. Each step along the journey brings the most beautiful colors possible through its power to heal and the privilege to practice it.

Then we moved into mending from any brokenness that has placed cracked spaces into our lives. What a sweet time of being raw and honest with who we are, where we see open gaps stitched up, gingerly stepped into the where and who of what we want to be in Christ! When we mend, we can then start the welcome task of binding and soothing, taking all those hurts, tying each one of them into our tapestry, interweaving them into the very fabric that will become you, will become me. No one else has that story, and that is beautiful, even though at times, we wish it was not ours.

Purposely Woven

I pray through these chapters you have chosen to evaluate and pause on just that – the fact that you are *unique* and *chosen*. You have a story to tell that no one else will *ever* have the privilege to share with the world. As we learn to embrace this truth, we are healed and can live a purpose-filled life. Owning, Mending, Binding must come before healing. We are reminded that healing takes precious time. No one can tell you how or when it should be completed. It's your process. If you choose to heal, you will! Forgiveness is a process that is ever-evolving as you heal. It will change its face and become more vibrant as it is weaved into your story.

Then we round out these pages with the beautiful task of restoration. My friend you have so much ability at your disposal. As you restore, you will metamorphose. You will blossom into someone who knows who they are and whom they serve! Can I say... I am so proud of you! I have walked this path with you, and I am well aware of the pain and sleepless nights it has created. You've asked God, "Really? Again?" You've shouted: "I can't do this anymore!" The beauty of our stories is that they will not be perfect. They will be filled with moments of incomprehension and intense heartbreak.

My heart hopes that these words were an encouragement to you on your journey, which my pain, heartache, and the spilling out of my soul was not in vain. If just one of you feels encouraged, then every hour spent writing was worth it. It sounds so strange to say, but I will anyway: I can see your faces; I can feel your hearts on some level. There is a connection from me to you. You have a purpose! Please take each color God has chosen to weave into your soul and make it brighter. Find your *why* here on earth. I believe so firmly that if each of us just took one of the trials we have gone through, asking Him to use it for good in our lives, we could impact the world! If each of us asked God, "How do you want me to use this [fill in the blank] for your kingdom and glory?" We would empower a generation to rise and change the very fabric of their tapestries! What is in your blank—a trial, sickness, broken relationship, abandonment, abuse, depression, addiction...? We all have a list and a story. Choose to ask how, and then be brave enough to take just one step towards what He speaks into it.

This call may be out of your comfort zone; yes, it most likely will be. We are not accustomed to being "uncomfortable." Here's the deal, friend: when we are comfortable, we don't grow. We just don't. God is calling all us broken vessels to be mighty warriors for Him. To speak up, walk out, start a movement, all in His name! Find your purpose! It's not as difficult as you think. God has already given you the colors, fabric, and tools. What excites or enrages you? What do you find yourself being passionate about? What mess has He *brought* you through that you can walk someone else through? What talent or burning desire has He gifted you with? Do you find yourself drawn to a certain cause or crowd of people, maybe an age group? It is right before your eyes, friend. Satan just likes to distract us with shiny objects that give us temporary satisfaction. He likes to fill our heads up with things that make us angry, that irritate. When we are focused on the problems and shortcomings of others, then we have no time to tend to our own.

With our minds distracted and confused, our hearts get tangled up, which draws us away from our purpose and potential. Why? Because he knows whom God uses: the most broken, and messy. The ones who feel they have made one too many mistakes and have missed their chance to be used by Him. God uses the humble and broken in ways we could never imagine! These precious ones are His army, friend. They are the few that seek to devour every Word He speaks, swimming in His grace. He bestows and know what it is like to live on the other side.

I am first in line in this dysfunctional group. I say, let's do this! It's time to take back our legacy and start believing that *broken is beautiful*. In the right hands, *broken* will flourish into the greatest story ever told. "God heals the brokenhearted and binds up their wounds," according to Psalm 147:3. He binds, heals, then gives you fresh wings to fly where He calls! He is waiting for you to believe it and choose Him.

Go out there and change the world! I can't wait to stand shoulder to shoulder with you and witness your colors. I *know* they will be mesmerizing.

In His Abundant Grace, Kele

Chapter Questions

1, My Weaving

At what moment in your life, did you recognize "this" could make or break *you?*

Debbie: The night I left secretly from my abusive husband. Also, the day I found out my present husband's mother had brain cancer. She was my "mother" figure.

Jennifer: There has been quite a lot of those moments. I think it would have been when I became pregnant with my son at age 20. Just coming out of a season of bad choices. I remember my dad asking me if I was ready to grow up. I said yes. So, there I was a single mom at 21. I felt the weight of being responsible for another person's life. That was the moment life got a bit more serious. I knew this was something that could make or break both of us!

Karen: October of 2016 when my son at age (22) lost his life in a tragic boating accident. It was his 11-month wedding anniversary. A black hole opened in my universe, sucking all my hopes and dreams into it. Adding to the sorrow was finding out that the driver of the boat (who was a family member) was intoxicated nearly three times over the legal limit that day.

2, Choosing the Weave

What "negatives" has your past been "woven" of?

Debbie: I feel there have been pain and darkness woven from fear, abandonment, illness, and loneliness.

Jennifer: My past story is woven of many negatives. Some were from other people sinning against me, but most of them where my own sins causing negative things in my life. A few things that have had a negative impact on my life. Was, being disobedient to my parents, premarital sex and the use of drugs. Which I think was at the heart of all my selfishness. The biggest "negative" was that I didn't recognize my need for God sooner. I have to say that even though I have had many negatives God used them all to lead me to Him!

Karen: Strands of dark and light that only God can see. My dark tones came from the unexpected death of my father, my journey through cancer (chemotherapy and baldness), the loss of my son, family members struggling through addictions, and my other son's divorce.

What was your moment of "enlightenment"? What does "Life Abundant" look like to you now versus your yesterday?

Debbie: I feel my moment of enlightenment has come from the verse God has spoken over my life, Joshua 1:9: "Have I not commanded you? Be strong and courageous. Do not be frightened; and do not be dismayed, for the Lord your God will be with you wherever you go."

Life today, versus my yesterday, is filled with blessings as I choose to see and enjoy what He gives me. John 10:10 tells us, "The thief comes only to steal and kill and destroy. I came so that they may have life and have it abundantly." The thief did come and destroy my first marriage. Yet, through our Father, the Great Restorer, I am now married to a godly man who is after God's heart.

Jennifer: My moment of enlightenment started when I heard the gospel and accepted Jesus Christ as my Savior. HE saved me by grace through faith. I began to realize I had a greater purpose. I began to look at life different.

My life of abundance is living my life in obedience to Christ. My abundance comes from knowing who I am in Christ. The past was full of things that couldn't satisfy. Yes, I had moments of happiness but not true abundance. The abundance didn't start until salvation.

Karen: I can say that my moment of enlightenment would be when I was ruminating over my son's death and the details of it. He died attempting to save the life of a 14-year-old family member on the same boat. I thought, "How would I respond in thanks to the parent who lost so much?" I was jolted into realization that this is exactly what Christ did! He gave His life to save my son. This Biblical truth became something very real and tangible for me, not just a theological concept.

Purposely Woven

Life abundant to me now is something I very eagerly look forward to. I look with new eyes into this world and see that life here is temporal, fleeting, passing away. The trinkets that adorn this world are mirages, made of tin. I have a confident hope of reconciliation.

3, Unraveling Grief

What advice can you give to us that you have learned from grieving? Was there a thought and/or area in which you were ever "stuck"?

Debbie: My advice would be that it is OK to rest in God. To ask Him to hold you. He truly knows and feels your grief. Try to remember that His timing is perfect, that rushing healing will not help. He is strong and capable. These verses walked me through deep hurt, reminding me that even when I may feel unreachable, He is there, holding me:

Purposely Woven

"The Lord is near to the brokenhearted and saves the crushed in spirit." Psalm 34:18

"You have kept count of my tossing's, put my tears in your bottle. Are they not in your book?" Psalm 56:8

I did find myself "stuck" in thinking that I was not worthy of being loved like the Lord told me I was loved. Particularly as a wife and mother.

Karen: As I was sucked into that deep black hole of my son's death, I was void of any colors. My mind had no safe haven in which to rest. Every thought was painful, every breath heart-tearing. I was not aware of it, but the other trials I had previously gone through were preparing me for a solid foundation I needed with God to endure this hole. I had no idea this foundation existed until the hurricane was breathing at my door. God reached up and spoke to me from His Word, Job 13:15a: "Though you slay me, yet I will trust you." I trusted Him and clung to Him with sheer desperation, fighting against the desire to die, give up, to "take the easy way out."

So my advice to another who is grieving: draw near to God, spend time getting to know Him, His truth, who you are in Christ. Let go of all beliefs that do not align with Scripture. Do it today! Tragedy comes without warning. God is strong enough to carry us through the valley, if we cling to Him and allow Him to do that. When we let go of His hand and venture

Purposely Woven

off on our own, we wander, making that time in the darkness longer than it needs to be.

4, Unraveling Denial

Was there ever an area/time of your life when shock or denial became a friend, welcomed or unwelcomed? What was your tool for overcoming this?

Debbie: Yes, when I was only married to my first husband for six months and I found out that He was having an affair. This was a time of deep denial for me. I was not a believer at the time, so the way I dealt with it, sadly, was by absorbing all the abuse and betrayal as a fault in me – that I was not a good wife.

Purposely Woven

Karen: Oh, yes, for the three days that I waited for the recovery of my son's body, shock and denial ran rampant through my mind. I was hoping that somehow, he would be alive, found somewhere. I just could not believe it was my son, our family, which this happened to.

My tool for hurdling these thoughts, was to look to God and what He promises. To trust Him... Really trust Him. For me this meant that God did not owe me an explanation. That His timing and plans unfold as He sees fit to unfold them. I had to remind myself that God is good, that He loves me. That is me trusting without reservation.

5, Unraveling the Bargain

Have you ever bargained with God? What choices, mentally or physically, did you make to overcome this desire to control the situation?

Debbie: Oh yes, many times. When my sweet mother-in-law was dying, I was so desperate to keep her that I would make promises to God. I would do all He asked me to if He would just heal my sweet Mary Jane. Through this time of walking Mary Jane through sickness, I saw her cling to her God. I was taught through her bold faith and from God that He does heal us. It just looks differently than we think at times. He can heal our bodies physically, yes. He has the power to do that. Yet He can also heal through wisdom we learn through an illness or by taking the hurting home to be with Him.

Jennifer: Yes, I have bargained with God. While having to move to a city that was not "home" for 3 years, I felt lost & wandering. I was ripped away from my church and community where I came to know Him... Why would He move me? I was fighting a battle to see what I wanted, what was comfortable for me. I wrestled and pleaded with God those 3 years. Yet, I knew the only way to overcome the desire to control the situation was to open Gods word and allow Him to change my heart and mind.

Karen: I don't know about bargaining but begging for sure. My desire to control a situation arises from making the choice to leave God out of the equation or circumstance. I will try to come up with plan A, B, and then C. All this comes from my overthinking, reasoning, or leaning on my own understanding. Some things that help me to overcome the need to control are keeping very close attention to what I am thinking about and trying *not* to lean on my own way of understanding. Here are verses that guide me into that thought process:

"Trust in the Lord with all your heart, and do not lean on your own understanding." Proverbs 3:5

Purposely Woven

"We destroy arguments and every lofty opinion raised against the knowledge of God and take every thought captive to obey Christ." 2 Corinthians 10:5

6, Untangling Darkness

Was there ever a time in your life when feelings dictated your decisions? Can you give advice on being raw and open with God and others in your life?

What is advice you would give to those struggling with the intimacy of prayer? What is one practice you implement to keep your prayer life connected?

Debbie: Yes, the first 10 years of my second and present marriage, I dealt with feelings of distrust. I was always looking to see if my husband was going to betray me. The truths I knew from the past told me he would. I used to pray for God to make my husband a great spiritual leader. Then one day God spoke and said, "I want you to pray that your husband becomes a man after me. I will take care of Him." So yes, my feelings were dictating even on how I prayed. I know that God knows all, and He loves and wants the very best for us. That we do not surprise Him with our thoughts. He knows those thoughts before we even speak. There is nothing we can hide from Him. There is gift and freedom in that knowledge.

One thing I try to practice is to ask for forgiveness as soon as I know I have sinned. I love to thank and praise Him through songs and worship as well.

Jennifer: My whole life before I knew Christ feelings dictated my decisions. Now that Christ is my foundation and who I look to for every decision, it's easy to be real and raw with others. Feelings don't define who I am, God does. Also knowing that God already knows everything about me. There is nothing to hide. If there is any place to be raw and real, it's before God. He died for all my sins. I know now that I will never hide anything from God. With people I can be raw and real because God has used all the negatives, failures and successes as part of my testimony, and all those things lead me to Jesus Christ as my Savior.

Regarding prayer; I would encourage anyone struggling with intimacy in prayer to remember who they are praying to and read the Word every day. Let the word teach you to pray. It's a choice we must make, to pray every day. If there is a lack of intimacy, it's not because of God it's because of us. It's hard to have intimacy when you don't spend time with someone. So, I would say press in even if at first, it's not comfortable. God's word says ""Ask and it will be given to you; seek and you will find; knock and the door will be opened to you. For everyone who asks receives; the one who seeks finds; and to the one who knocks, the door will be opened. Matthew 7:7-8 NIV Seek Him in prayer He is faithful to be found.

Karen: When I was younger, feelings dominated my life, for sure. Even as a Christian wife and mother, I allowed my feelings to have free reign, accepting that was the "female way." I have since learned that operating off my feelings has landed me in trouble and still can. It can wound others I love and those I encounter. This seems for me to be a place where the enemy likes to wreak havoc in my life. I must start to recognize that not every thought in my mind is from God. I must learn to pause and be still, listen for God to guide my thought process. Considering God in the "feeling" is not always easy, but it is always right. I try to stop and ask,

"Are the words I am about to speak or the action I might take be pleasing and honoring to *me* or God?"

Regarding prayer, the word tells us that God wants a relationship with us. This cannot be accomplished by me doing all the talking and God doing all the listening. Or me giving Him a "to do" list. The Holy Spirit wants to minister to my heart; I must take time to listen and be still. I feel God most when I make this effort. God is all around me, in me, yet I will only see this when I quiet my heart, my day, and wait, abide, and dwell in Him.

7, Untangling Anger

What is your "wait on the Lord"? Have you ever struggled with anger or blame towards yourself or others? Has there been a "wait in the Lord season in your life"? How have you chosen to not befriend it anger or blame?

Jennifer: I struggled with anger for a long time. The crazy thing was I didn't realize how angry I was till the Lord started to work it out of me. The self-blame would always come after the anger. I would blame myself for not being able to control my tongue or this rage I would sometimes feel. I would fall to my knees so many times asking God to help me to not be angry. I continued to open Gods word and believe what it was saying and that it was teaching me. Without reading the truth it's easy to believe lies. I chose to listen to the voice of God and let His Word do what it says it will do by the power of the Holy Spirit. By being obedient to what Scripture says by the power of the Holy Spirt those behaviors will fade away and be replaced.

"Therefore, do not let sin reign in your mortal body so that you obey its evil desires. Do not offer any part of yourself to sin as an instrument of wickedness, but rather offer yourselves to God as those who have been brought from death to life; and offer every part of yourself to him as an instrument of righteousness. For sin shall no longer be your master, because you are not under the law, but under grace." Romans 6:12-14 NIV

Purposely Woven

Karen: I feel my wait at this point in my life is heaven. This is not my home, and there will never be a time in this world when everything "works out." I can say that when my son died and we later found out the details surrounding the accident (intoxication), I was experiencing anger that I did not know what to do with. A grief counselor spoke this over me: "The Bible does not tell us not to be angry; it says be angry but do not sin" (Ephesians 4:26). He then led me into some ways to let my anger "leak" from me. I wrote a letter to the man who was the subject of my anger. Through the process of weeping and venting, I was reminded that Christ died for this man, too. Christ offers forgiveness to *all*. I can do the same. I can combat anger or blame when I don't let it fester in my heart or mind as "background noise." James 4:7 says, "Therefore submit to God. Resist the devil and he will flee from you." I must do the resisting, which means being conscious of my thoughts and aware of Satan's schemes.

8, Threading Acceptance

What is one lesson/wisdom regarding acceptance you have learned from the trials you have endured?

Karen: To find an outlet for expressing your sorrow, heartache, or disappointment. For me that is in writing a journal entry or letter. I have hiked to a hilltop to weep and pray. I have prayed for loved ones and buried a mustard seed as a visual reminder of the small amount of faith it takes to move mountains (Matthew 17:20). Find a ritual that connects you to God and allow Him to comfort you.

9, Threading Release

Have you dealt with labels and or lies placed upon you? Is there a scripture or truth you cling to for healing in this area?

Debbie: There was a time I was in a job that had many political demands on it. I did not have the education, experience, or talents for this position. I am not an eloquent speaker and have problems pronouncing certain words. During this time, I had many instances where I would receive letters mailed to my desk with clippings to attend speech school. This was hurtful, and I wanted to give up. But God clearly stated to me that He placed me here and He would give me the words to speak and the strength and

Purposely Woven

wisdom to do the job before me. There were times I wanted to give up, but these Scriptures walked me through:

"For the Holy Spirit will teach you in that very hour what you ought to say." Luke 12:12

"Not by the way of eye-service, as people pleasers, but as servants of Christ, doing the will of God from the heart." Ephesians 6:6

Karen: The tragedy that took our son rocked our small community. There was an addiction that was not addressed and in turn took three lives. A year and a half after the accident, false information was brought forth publicly. God asked me to respond with truth to these claims. What followed were backlash and accusations that were shocking and overwhelming. God reminded me through this hurt that "I could not turn these stones into bread." I needed to seek spiritual nourishment, not acceptance from others. God led me to Ecclesiastes 3, which elaborates on the fact that there is a season for everything – to be born, to die, to gain and to lose, to be silent and to speak. I had done what He instructed; now I was to let Him do the rest.

10, Method of Mending

Can you share with us one thing the Lord has restored that you were in "wait" for?

Based on your mending journey, what is one piece of advice you can pass along?

Debbie: I have had my trust in people restored, but especially in my close relationships, like my husband. He has allowed me to take all the baggage from my past and wrap it up through restoration with forgiveness, trust, gentleness, and kindness. Letting God choose my new mate instead of me controlling the choosing was worth it.

Jennifer: The Lord has mended my relationship with Him. This is the thing I am most thankful for. My advice would be to always focus on the Lord, His Word and His faithfulness.

Karen: For years I was in wait for my husband to have a more living, active relationship with the Lord. Through the loss of our son, God has brought my husband to that very place. In fact, my husband wonders if he was ever a Christian before this. God promises to bring beauty from ashes. Isaiah 61:3 says, "To give those who mourn a beautiful headdress instead of ashes, the oil of gladness instead of mourning, the garment of praise instead of a faint spirit." The blessings *are* there if we choose to see them.

Purposely Woven

Remember how much you are loved by God. He desires the best for you and loves you!

11, Method of Binding

How has releasing your hurt to God given you freedom in your daily life? Was there a challenge in this for you?

Debbie: As I release bitterness and hurt that has walked into my life, I feel the weight of stress fall from me. The challenge I struggle with is control. I felt like if I could just control everything, I could change the outcome of others' actions. This lie is straight from the enemy. My wall was trusting again. I know that the Bible says all will turn out for my good. Yet some turns did not feel like light, but darkness. Trusting God when you want to control starts off scary, yet our faith grows deep roots when we let God have complete control.

Jennifer: Releasing hurt over to the Lord is the only way to have true freedom. The freedom is found in HIM alone. Honestly, I think every time the Lord has asked me to relinquish my flesh to walk in obedience to Him it's a challenge. I can always feel the battle within myself. The Spirit of God is guiding me, but also my flesh wants to do what I used to do. It has does get easier over time. The closer I get to the Lord the more my desire to live in the flesh fades. As I walk in the Spirit honoring God with the life, HE has given me is where freedom is. The sacrifice He made in paying the penalty for the sins of the world... How could I not respond by laying all my life down to HIM hurts and all.

Karen: Taking my thoughts captive, binding them and releasing control over to God has literally SAVED my life. It can be very challenging and daunting at times to practice being conscious of every thought. Yet it does not take long to see the results and to feel the freedom of not being held captive by the fear, hurt, sadness, rejection, and grief. The enemy does not want us to know the truth that we CAN walk in victory.

12, Intertwine Healing

On your path to forgiveness, what helped guide you to wholeness, breaking your chains?

Jennifer: I forgive because Christ forgave me. That is always what the Lord brings to my mind. Through the process of Him changing me, I see how much Christ has forgiven me. Which makes it easier to forgive others. Even when it's not easy and in my flesh, I struggle, I know that Jesus Christ will work that out in me. In Christ all those chains are broken, only in Him do I find wholeness.

Karen: For me it was the realization that, to receive God's forgiveness, it is imperative for me to extend that to others. Christ is clear about the consequences of unforgiveness in Matthew 18:21-35. It has not always been an easy path for me. But it is a crucial element for me if I want to stay free of bondage and bitterness.

Purposely Woven

13, Weaving Restoration

How has your path of restoration played a role in your daily life and relationships?

Debbie: Freedom in "letting go and letting God," reminds me that He is the One who knows me, my past, present, and future. He guides me, and I am never alone. I am reminded that He wants the very best for me and that this restoring continues every day I get to walk on this earth.

Karen: My relationship with God is closer than it has ever been. Even though I am moving into another season of loss, with family dynamics changing, I am reminded more and more than I cannot survive this life and its struggles without the Lord. I take great comfort in the promises of 2 Corinthians 4:17-18: "For this light momentary affliction is preparing for us an external weight of glory beyond all comparison, as we look not to the things that are seen but to the things that are unseen. For the things that are seen are transient, but the things that are unseen are eternal."

Closing, You're Weaving

What has God revealed in your pain as your purpose?

What advice would you give others on finding purpose in their life journey?

Debbie: My purpose has become to encourage others. To share my story of God's glory, love, and mercy through all the pain of my past and the deliverance from it through Him. I would advise you to stay close to God. If you see busyness or distractions getting in the way of that, good or bad, quickly switch directions so that God is your highest priority. Hebrews

4:12 says, "For the word of God is living and active. Sharper than any two-edged sword, piercing to the division of soul and of spirit, of joints and of marrow, and discerning the thoughts and the intentions of the heart." Learn to wield your sword skillfully, actively, and intentionally!

Jennifer: God has absolutely revealed that HE is the purpose, not my pain. There is one certain pain/trial that has been ongoing since I became a believer. It's just one thing the Lord has used to sanctify me. The trial has so many purposes. I can always believe what the word says, even if I don't understand the why. I know God is always good and that HIS ways are higher than my own (Isaiah 55:8-9)

Purposely Woven

1 Peter 1:6-7 NASB says "In this you greatly rejoice, even though now for a little while, if necessary, you have been distressed by various trials, so that the proof of your faith, being more precious than gold which is perishable even though tested by fire, maybe found to result in praise and glory and honor at the revelation of Jesus Christ"

James 1:2-4 NASB says "Consider it all joy, my brethren, when you encounter various trials, knowing that the testing of your faith produces endurance. And let endurance have its perfect result, so that you may be perfect and complete, lacking in nothing."

So, I would encourage you to believe what the Word of God says. Make that the focus of your heart and mind in your trials. Let bringing honor and glory to God be your purpose in every situation. When you are focused on Christ, trials and tragedies will always become triumphs!

Karen: This new chapter in my life has given me new depth to my compassion. I am able to come alongside those who are hurting, struggling, searching, through ministry work that I love. I am able to discuss how God has walked me through any parent's worst nightmare, holding me close, being ever faithful to His promises. I also blog my journey to plant seeds for others walking in the darkness of loss.

My advice: God will give you a purpose that resonates with your soul and brings joy to your heart. He rewards those who seek Him (Hebrews 11:6b). His yoke is easy, and His burden is light (Matthew 11:30). That yoke is like Christ putting His arm around your shoulder and walking with you, side by side. Be still and listen to what He speaks into your life.